Papier-Mâché Treasures

with Teena Flanner

Papier-Mâché Treasures

with Teena Flanner

Creating Your Own Vintage-Style Collectibles

LARK BOOKS

A Division of Sterling Publishing Co., Inc.

New York / London

A Red Lips 4 Courage Communications, Inc. book
www.redlips4courage.com
Eileen Cannon Paulin, *President*
Catherine Risling, *Director of Editorial*

Editor
Catherine Risling

Photographer
Zachary Williams
Williams Visual

Copy Editor
Lecia Monsen

Photo Stylist
Erika Kotite

Book Designer
Dori Dixon
D3Grafx, Inc.

Library of Congress Cataloging-in-Publication Data

Flanner, Teena, 1946-
Papier mache treasures with Teena Flanner : creating your own vintage-style collectibles / author, Teena Flanner. — 1st ed.
p. cm.
Includes index.
ISBN-13: 978-1-60059-172-3 (hc-plc with jacket : alk. paper)
ISBN-10: 1-60059-172-8 (hc-plc with jacket : alk. paper)
1. Papier-mâché. I. Title.
TT871.F53 2007
745.54'2 — dc22
2007011106

10 9 8 7 6 5 4 3 2 1

First Edition

Published by Lark Books,
A Division of Sterling Publishing Co., Inc.
387 Park Avenue South, New York, NY 10016

Text © 2007, Teena Flanner
Photography © 2007, Red Lips 4 Courage
Communications, Inc.

Distributed in Canada by Sterling Publishing,
c/o Canadian Manda Group, 165 Dufferin Street
Toronto, Ontario, Canada M6K 3H6
Distributed in the United Kingdom by
GMC Distribution Services, Castle Place,
166 High Street, Lewes, East Sussex, England BN7 1XU

Distributed in Australia by Capricorn Link
(Australia) Pty Ltd., P.O. Box 704, Windsor,
NSW 2756 Australia

The written instructions, photographs, designs, patterns, and projects in this volume are intended for the personal use of the reader and may be reproduced for that purpose only. Any other use, especially commercial use, is forbidden under law without written permission of the copyright holder.

Every effort has been made to ensure that all the information in this book is accurate. However, due to differing conditions, tools, and individual skills, the publisher cannot be responsible for any injuries, losses, and other damages that may result from the use of the information in this book.

If you have questions or comments about this book, please contact:
Lark Books
67 Broadway
Asheville, NC 28801
(828) 253-0467

Manufactured in China

ISBN 10: 1-60059-172-8
ISBN 13: 978-1-60059-172-3

For information about custom editions, special sales, premium and corporate purchases, please contact Sterling Special Sales Department at (800) 805-5489; or e-mail specialsales@sterlingpub.com.

"Every child is an artist, the problem is how to remain an artist once one is grown."

— *Pablo Picasso*

Contents

Introduction

My earliest papier-mâché project was a tortoise and hare I made when I was eight years old. The figures were formed from wads of paper shaped like Aesop's characters and covered with strips of paper and a thick mixture of simple glue made with flour and water. I used toothpicks for the tortoise's legs, shaped little floppy rabbit ears with my hands, and painted one figure blue with white posies and the other white with blue posies.

Other school-day projects were crafted with air-filled balloons and strips of newspaper, flour, and water. They were inexpensive, non-toxic, and lightweight and painted with poster paint. This is still the process that comes to many people's mind when papier-mâché is mentioned.

While still rudimentary and very hands-on, papier-mâché has become my livelihood and a great source of enjoyment. I have made hundreds of glittering figures, each with its own personality, that have become sought-after collectibles. With a few basic materials and techniques outlined on the following pages, you can create your very own vintage-inspired beauties.

The tools for my work are simple; it is the creativity and experience that is important. Each piece is one-of-a-kind even though it is made from a mold. Not until the last detail is complete does the unique personality appear. This is a satisfying moment for me.

Many different cultures have used papier-mâché to make dolls, puppets, toys, and holiday decorations.

My very first papier-mâché pieces, made from chalkware molds, were quite serious. Four years after making the first pieces, I added glitter which has become my trademark.

Halloween collectibles of witches, goblins, and other spooky creatures are often made of papier-mâché and coated with a thin layer of plaster or formed from composition, which is partially paper. Often the pieces are hollow and the heads lift off so candy and treats can be placed inside.

The most recognizable icon of the Halloween holiday is perhaps the hollow, pressed-cardboard jack-o'-lantern, which is just another form of papier-mâché. These pieces were originally made in Germany in the first part of the 20th century by cottage craftspeople and then as late as the 1950s in Japan. Vintage Santa Clauses and stern Belsnickles were sometimes formed with a papier-mâché head and a body of wood, and then dressed in fabric. Often the entire figures were crafted of papier-mâché, painted with beautiful rich colors and produced in limited numbers. Today, these are desirable collectibles.

I love both the papier-mâché process and the finished products. I've worked with papier-mâché for more than two decades. My shelves are lined with molds, old and new, and vintage snippets of silk, faded millinery, antique tinsel, and other treasures, all of which inspire new collections of figures.

I hope you venture into my world of papier-mâché, where creating figures is fun and embellishing them is even more satisfying.

Teena Flanner

Chapter 1

Getting Started

A rt materials inspire me. I have large quantities of supplies and materials, both new and vintage. Sterling tinsel trim, velvet ribbon, old holly leaves, faded millinery flowers—I collect them all. Each piece in my collection either inspires a project already in mind or an idea somewhere down the road.

Each embellishment adds a nostalgic touch to my pieces. I love layering elements, taking something pretty and using it to dress up my papier-mâché treasures inspired by the past.

For anyone interested in embarking on papier-mâché projects, there are a few basic supplies to have on hand. But remember, this art form is not an exact science; working with papier-mâché takes a lot of experimenting.

I can't tell you the exact measurements for water or the exact amount of dry papier-mâché mix; I can only suggest a starting point. Working with papier-mâché is much like baking; simply add "a little of this and a little of that" to get the right consistency.

All of the ingredients used in making papier-mâché figures are evironmentally sound and most ingredients are water-based.

Setting up Your Workshop

Oilcloth, a vinyl window shade, or a clean shower curtain will protect surfaces from liquids, spills, glue, and the papier-mâché itself. Everything I use should inspire me so I search for bright pinks, creamy whites, and spunky nostalgic prints. I even change my cloths each season because I believe the creative process should be fun. These coverings will protect the work area and will ensure that the figure doesn't stick to the surface, which is very important.

Materials

Papier-mâché

The projects featured throughout this book are irregular figures. I can list a precise amount of water to add, but the dry mix is fluffy and differs in packing density, measuring, humidity, and even the age of the dry mix itself. Before you begin any project, purchase a minimum of two 3-pound bags of dry papier-mâché compound mix that has a set-up time of 30 minutes. Be experimental. If there is more than one variety available, buy one of each. You will soon have a favorite mixture. Each type has benefits but is quite different in its qualities. About 36 pounds makes 1 cubic foot of dry papier-mâché mixture so you can see the difficulty of specific amounts with the variations in the shape of each figure.

You may certainly make your own mixture, and I love to experiment. Easy-to-follow recipes are readily available online.

Homemade mixes contain paper pulp, which needs to be mixed with cellulose, glues, wallpaper paste, sawdust, or plaster. These additives aid drying time, and without them your figure will sour before it can be removed from the mold. In general, though, I opt for store-bought papier-mâché mixes.

Acrylic paint

Although my primary paints are acrylic, I often use latex paint from a leftover home project. White latex acts like gesso as it smoothes the surface texture of a project a bit. When glaze is applied over dried latex, the aged patina effect is more pronounced than when using acrylic paint.

Feel free to experiment. The variety of colors available in acrylics is inspiring. Still, I often soften a color to make it just the hue and shade I desire.

Glitter

When I began working in papier-mâché, the variety of glitter choices was limited; most available glitter was the sort used for school projects. Today, glitter is widely available in all sorts of sizes—from ultra-fine to chunky—and in a wide range of exquisite, breathtaking colors.

Beautiful, nostalgic German glass glitter in rich colors and sized from very fine to coarse is available from several online retail sites. I sometimes apply glass glitter using a clear-drying blue gel glue found at many craft stores. Glass glitter is not translucent and will completely cover the surface to which it is applied. Since my pieces are always painted with details, this opaque glitter is pretty for accents only. It is exquisite and authentic but proceed with caution; after all, it is glass.

Ultra-fine glitters are available in an amazing array of colors. Best part is, a little goes a very long way. This lovely product is not transparent and will hide the painting on the figure, so I sprinkle it on with a very light hand. I always use diluted white craft glue to adhere these glitters. With papier-mâché, undiluted glue can remain visible after dried, in spite

of the "dries clear" labeling. Under the crystal or snow glitter, any visible glue adds to the "frostiness." With ultra-fine glitter, the visible dried glue is undesirable.

When applying glitter to figures, it is helpful to have squares of wax paper on hand. Glitter the piece over the wax paper so the extra can be collected and returned to the glitter container, or mix leftover colors together to create a new shade that can be used on other projects.

The old-fashioned, coarser elementary school glitters should not be forgotten. Along with doilies, red construction paper, and scissors, Valentine's Day memories make this glitter the most nostalgic of them all. This coarser metallic, opaque glitter comes in a delectable lime green and pale blue, and classics like silver, gold, and red.

Water

When working, keep a pitcher of water nearby. Papier-mâché is messy and the more you can contain your tools and supplies, the less mess will be tracked through your workspace. A glass of water for rinsing your brush is also necessary.

White craft glue

Paintbrushes

Measuring tools

White craft glue

Craft glue is used as a base for adhering most of my glitters. When using white craft glue, plunge your craft brush in water immediately after gluing is completed and clean thoroughly; blot with a paper towel. Dried papier-mâché pieces that need repair should be fixed with white craft glue.

Paintbrushes

Buy an inexpensive package of paintbrushes that contains an assortment of sizes. Sets should include a No. 0 fine liner and No. 4, 5, and 6 round brushes. Also used in most projects are craft brushes in sizes 1" and 1½". These brushes, also named "chip" brushes, are handy for painting larger surfaces and applying glue. When they become too stiff, just throw them away. Some other things to keep in mind when it comes to brushes:

* Acrylic paints are tougher on bristles than oil paints so make sure you purchase synthetic brushes.
* Clean brushes immediately after painting as acrylics dry quickly. Use a mild dish detergent and room-temperature water to clean the paintbrushes and prolong their useful life.
* Reshape the point of the brush while the bristles are wet. Never allow brushes to stand in a jar of water.

Measuring Tools

In projects that combine wet and dry elements, the dry materials should be measured first. Duplicates of measuring tools will make this easier. I like a plastic tablespoon because it can be used to stir and smooth the wet mixture. I mix the papier-mâché with my hands as it is easier to judge its consistency.

Each project lists measurements, which are to be used as a starting point. You will quickly learn the most effective consistency. If you have made too much papier-mâché, use the excess for a tiny, hand-molded project. If you make too little, whip up a bit more mixture.

Around the House

In addition to an oven, some basic items that are required for nearly every project in this book include:

* Ceramic, plastic, or glass bowl (1 quart or larger)
* Colander or sifter
* Cooking spray
* Dishwashing liquid
* Large metal or wooden mixing spoon
* Lint-free cloth
* Measuring cups
* Measuring spoons
* Paper cups
* Paper towels
* Paring knife
* Pitcher of water (1 quart or larger)
* Small glass jars with lids
* Wax paper

Working with Papier-mâché

Creating with papier-mâché is about experimenting and nurturing your creativity. The proper consistency is learned, starting with my basic measurements.

It is not the easiest medium but it is one of the most forgiving. Repairs and alterations can be made anytime, when wet or even after the piece has dried and is painted. I always use my hands because I love the tactile quality of the entire process.

With most molds, I form a slurry as the first layer. This has a thin, watery consistency and allows the papier-mâché to sink into the details of the mold. The slurry should be runny but with enough substance to hold onto the walls of the mold. It is approximately 1 part dry papier-mâché mix, 1 part water.

When the slurry becomes firm, the second and final layer is made using a proportion of 2 parts dry papier-mâché mix, 1 part water. This firmer consistency will give the piece support. It is important to keep the slurry away from the top edges of the mold, where the two halves will be joined. This area needs to be filled with the final layer so the pieces will join when clamping the mold together.

Choose a large bowl that will be allocated to hold only papier-mâché. Keep this bowl clean, as remainders of dry papier-mâché will cause the new mixture to set too quickly. Keep a colander or sifter on your work surface to filter the paper from the water, and keep all papier-mâché away from your drain.

10 Things to Remember When Making Papier-mâché Mixture

1. **Choose mixture carefully.** Select a dry pre-made compound that combines the best features of papier-mâché, clay, and old-fashioned plaster. Another method, which was also hollow, was a mixture of plaster and papier-mâché. This was called composition. Don't be concerned if it has added ingredients; it is still papier-mâché.

2. **Learn not to answer the phone.** Papier-mâché mixtures set quickly. Mix enough to be used within 15 minutes.

3. **Clean often.** Hardened papier-mâché acts as a catalyst and will cause your fresh batch to dry quickly, so keep your molds, mixing bowl, and utensils clean.

4. **Press firmly.** A plastic measuring tablespoon is a wonderful tool for pressing mixture into a mold; your fingers are even better. It's important to press papier-mâché firmly into the crevices of the mold to achieve all of the details.

5. **Proportion is important.** If you're creating slurry, your mixture should be very wet. Your second layer will be stiffer.

6. **Remember, paper pulp is fluffy.** All measurements in the projects throughout this book are approximate. There is no substitute for experience and no way to obtain experience without just getting in there and doing it. Humidity, the firmness of packing the pulp when measuring, and even the age of the paper mixture all affect the outcome of your mixture.

7. **Watch for water accumulation.** If after 30 minutes water from the slurry has risen to form a pool, gently blot with a paper towel.

8. **Keep mix in a bag.** Keep unmixed papier-mâché away from moisture, sealed in a plastic bag.

9. **Trash it.** Never put scraps of papier-mâché mixture down the drain or you will clog your system. Pour any unclear water through a large wire mesh sifter or fine colander. This retains the solids, which can be placed in the wastebasket while allowing the water to go down the drain.

10. **Love the process and the finished product.** Don't strive for perfection—that is not the goal. Be patient with both yourself and your medium. Each piece should reflect your personal touch.

Working with Molds

Metal Molds

Original metal molds were usually made in several graduated sizes. There are thousands of shapes and sizes, all with their own story and history.

The French and Germans were known for their intricate molds. They were created by extremely talented artists who would first create a design in plaster. A very detailed metal mold was then made by sand casting. Cut in half, the original plaster piece was pressed into the sand and then removed. Molten metal was poured into the impressions, creating a positive exactly like the original. From this piece a tin mold was formed with high pressure to ensure each delicate detail.

When a mold is used to make a chocolate or papier-mâché figure, in a way, it is returning to the original production method—filling details in the interior of the mold with chocolate or papier-mâché much as the molten metal was poured into the sand.

After cleaning your mold, a bit of rust is normal. It can be removed with an abrasive pad, rinsed, and dried thoroughly. Practice using mold clips or rubber bands to secure the mold halves before beginning a project. Some clips are tricky and papier-mâché won't wait to set.

You may want to use metal molds only once for papier-mâché as the mixture is damaging to the metal. These molds were created for chocolate with its high fat content. The rare vintage molds add a lovely, authentic touch to holiday collections displayed in cupboards or on tabletops. The old silvery color, texture, and variety of shapes and sizes make the molds valued collectibles.

Plastic Molds

Plastic molds, first produced in the 1960s and still made today, are not as pretty as metal molds but they are practical, easily obtainable, and durable when used with papier-mâché. Readily available in candy shops, they are available in designs that are exact copies of historic pieces and also contemporary figures. I miss the beauty and the wonderful details of metal molds but it is comforting to know that I am not damaging a beautiful antique with my art. So I use and collect all types of molds.

There are flat and three-dimensional molds in contemporary and vintage styles. My favorites are the new molds copied exactly from vintage metal molds. Some plastic molds have large, flat borders surrounding the figure. This makes it a challenge to align the two halves of the figure when it's filled with an opaque mixture.

Before beginning a project with plastic molds, it is helpful to first outline the figure. Place only one half of the mold, open side down, on your work surface. Outline the figure shape with a brightly colored, medium-tipped permanent marker. This will help you line up both sides of the figure when the mold is filled.

Pewter Molds

Some of the molds in my collection are pewter and were created for ice cream. These old molds are very heavy, and the halves are permanently attached with heavy clasps. These are often made with multiple cavities of the same figure. I have rabbits, a groom, and even Humpty Dumpy in pewter ice cream molds.

Techniques

Making a Gel Mold

What you'll need:

* ½ cup gel molding compound
* ¾ cup water
* Cooking spray
* Fork
* Medium-size bowl
* Original figure
* Paper cup
* Paring knife
* Scissors

Making molds can be a daunting task but to gain mastery, begin with this easier method. A simple, smaller figure works best when making a gel mold. The amounts given below are for a small turkey, 2" x 2½". To measure for a different figure, find a container (ideally something you can tear away, such as a paper cup) at least ¼" larger than your original figure on all sides. Pour water into container and that amount will be the correct measurement of water.

For every 1 cup of loosely packed gel compound, you need 1½ cups of water;

be sure to adjust for the size of your container and original figure.

Choose a container in a size and shape that is at least ¼" larger than the figure on all sides. For a small turkey, I used an 8-ounce paper cup, and cut it with scissors to a height ¼" taller than the figure. Stir for 1 minute; the compound will set in 2 minutes. Using cooler water will allow you more time.

For easy mold release, prepare your figure and rinse with cool water or use a thin coat of cooking spray. This mold can be used 3–4 times.

What you'll do:

1.  In medium-size bowl, mix water and gel compound gently and quickly whisk with a fork until smooth, like thick crepe batter.

2.  Immediately pour mixture into your container.

3.  Plunge figure into container; do not completely submerge. The base should be bare. Hold completely still for 1–2 minutes until hardened.

4. 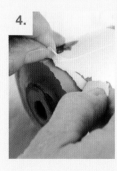 Remove figure from mold. Often the figure will not easily release due to undercuts. With your paring knife, cut completely through mold from base, over figure and back to base.

5. 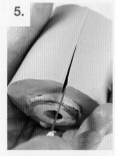 Using paring knife, slice one side of mold and remove original figure.

6.  Use this mold the same as a plastic, metal, or silicone mold, using a rubber band to hold the mold closed. This mold cannot be cleaned as it will dissolve.

Making a Silicone Mold

When making a silicone mold, I recommend using a two-part compound. This is good for figures with deep undercuts. It is flexible for the removal of both the original figure and the subsequent figures you will make. This compound produces a durable mold good for many castings.

Silicones are measured by weight, 10 parts base by weight to 1 part activator by weight. The typical manufacturer-recommended process needs to be de-aerated in a vacuum chamber at 26"–29" of mercury vacuum.

Hobbyists do not generally have this equipment. I skip the mercury vacuum; however, bubbles in the mold can occur at an important spot. If this occurs, I repair and sculpt the papier-mâché figure when it's removed from the silicone mold.

What you'll need:

* 2-part compound
* Hot-glue gun and glue sticks
* Metal fork
* Original figure
* Paper towel
* Petroleum jelly
* Protective gear (as specified on epoxy label)
* Scale
* Wood box

What you'll do:

1.  Cover figure and inside of box with a thin coating of petroleum jelly. The figure will be hot glued next so do not apply petroleum jelly to bottom base of original or the bottom of box.

2. 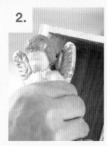 Stand the box upright. Hot glue original standing in center of bottom of box. Make certain there is at least 1" behind and in front of original for the silicone.

3.  Calculate approximate volume to cover half of master. *Note:* Silicone is 2 parts mixed by weight, 1 part activator, 10 parts base. Weighing and proportion must be exact.

4.  Weigh, pour, and mix proper amounts of blue activator and white base with a fork in a plastic container. Incorporate as few bubbles as possible into mixture.

5.  Once activator and base touch, working time is 20–30 minutes including mixing and pouring time. Stir until a uniform color results, with no streaks of white or blue.

6.  Carefully pour the catalyzed silicone rubber (the sum of the 2 parts) around original until half is covered. Let cure 16–18 hours until firm and not sticky.

7. When silicone has cured, spread petroleum jelly on newly cured and exposed surfaces. Repeat above steps for second half of process. Fill past the figure, all the way level to the top. Let cure 16–18 hours and then remove sides of box and master.

8. 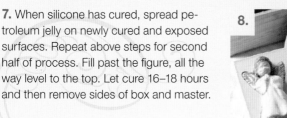 Mold will be two parts and finely detailed. Wait another 16 hours before using mold.

Trimming Papier-Mâché Figures

The natural characteristics of papier-mâché are some of the qualities that first attracted me to this medium. Each piece, though made from the same mold, is unique. A Santa's belly will slip, the height of a second figure will be different, and each little face is never quite the same.

When I trim a molded figure that has set, I want to keep these inherent qualities. I don't aim for perfection. Each one needs a lovely face and a steady stance, and no missing features. Since they are formed from a mold, each figure will have a seam. I hold a small paring knife at a 45-degree angle and remove most of the seam. The molds are charming and the process should not be erased so I make no attempt to remove and disguise the entire seam.

Making Repairs

When removing a figure from its mold, sometimes you may lose some of the detailing. Missing details can be fixed because papier-mâché is not an exact medium, and you can be lenient with the details. Repairs are made by filling in the damage with wet papier-mâché scraps and placing the figure back into the mold to solidify the features.

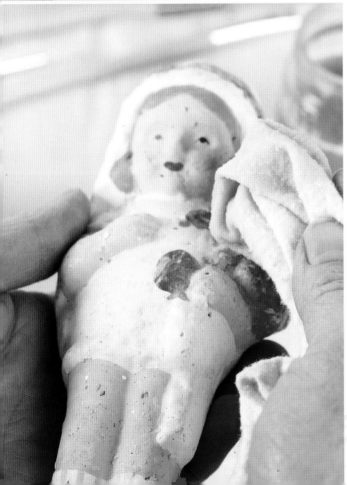

Painting Figures

Papier-mâché provides an uneven surface for painting. This makes it an inexact art and I find it more creative and forgiving than a more consistent surface. I aim for character; I know the personality of the figure I have created and I want that uniqueness to be evident in the final product. Perfection is not my goal.

When painting flowers, I usually dip the pointed tip of my brush into more than one color without rinsing. For a rose, I dip just the tip into red paint, and then dip it deeper into white or cream paint. I rarely use any color straight from the bottle; mixing can be done on a small dish or palette. This will help preserve bottled colors.

I am very particular about faces—both the papier-mâché form and the painting. Cheeks must be pale and rosy; mouths are small and friendly; and eyes add to the overall character of the piece. With some projects, I draw the eyes with a very pointed liner brush. With others, I wait until all steps of the project, except glittering, are completed and the figure is thoroughly dry before I draw the eyes with an ultra-fine permanent marker.

Unless noted in the instructions, let paint dry after each application before moving on to the next step.

Glazing Figures

To soften the raw qualities of the papier-mâché, meld paint colors, and to achieve the look of a wonderfully aged patina, glaze is painted on each figure before glittering. Simply mix water, a colorant, and faux glaze medium and rub gently over entire figure with a soft cloth. The glaze will also highlight the tiny nooks and crannies of the figure.

ARTIST'S notes
Glittering Made Easy

When working with crystal glitter, I use a cardboard box that is the size of the papier-mâché figure. The figure, still wet from gluing, can be rolled in the sparkly particles for easy application.

Glittering Figures

My favorite glitter is the crystal, which can frost a piece, mimicking snow and ice, or lend a sugar-coated appearance perfect for springtime figures. Crystal glitter is also lovely as sugar on eggs and rabbits. I suggest that you have a ¼-pound container of crystal glitter in your work area. It is my primary glitter.

I have used mica, which is lovely for a wintry, antique look. These pearlized flakes were used a lot in the 1950s.

I also love the look of chunky glass glitter and use it sparingly. It is glass, so be careful when working with it.

Colored glass glitters are opaque, and I sometimes use a blue school glue for securing this old-fashioned glitter. Carefully pat glitter onto the wet glue and let dry.

I use diluted and undiluted white craft glue depending on the project, almost always applied with a craft brush. A paper cup is a handy glue container because the opening is wide enough for a brush. When I have finished, I can dispose of the cup and the leftover glue so my drain is spared. If I am working on multiple projects, I pour glue into a glass jar and seal it with a lid between each use.

Ultra-fine colored glitters are more expensive but go a long way. Weights of containers vary as do makers but ½ ounce of ultra-fine glitter for each project is ample. Amazingly enough, this tiny amount can embellish several projects.

Embellishing Figures

Once your papier-mâché figure has its own personality, now it's time for some real fun.

I like to use meaningful flourishes from my childhood, such as a velvet flower from one of my springtime bonnets. A tiny bell or a charm threaded onto a velvet ribbon works wonderfully as a dog collar. The colors of old, faded embellishments add appeal to my papier-mâché figures. Vintage snippets of velvet, luscious double-faced satin ribbon, slightly bent sprigs of faux holly, and tarnished sterling tinsel garlands are beautiful adornments.

ARTIST'S notes
Lessons in Vintage

Educate yourself as to what makes an item appear vintage. Is it the color or the form? If an item is impossible to locate, can the look be captured with something new?

To begin your homework, study old pieces. Learn to appreciate the colors, textures, and shapes of estate-sale and antique finds. When you get a feel for what is vintage, roam the aisles of a craft store. You will be inspired by at least one item or material on each visit.

For years, I have kept an eye out for lovely vintage ribbons, faded crepe paper, and odd notions. Years after large stores have discontinued taffeta ribbons, shops and fabric stores in small towns may still have an ample supply in their dry goods departments.

Oilcloth, with patterns long discontinued, may still be in stock in these off-the-beaten-track variety stores. The sun will fade crepe paper in a few weeks so items for the window display that have been in the store for a long time are often under-appreciated by others. Supplies and embellishments collected before I need them inspire my work.

Chapter 2

Spring

Spring's colors are so welcoming. The yellow–greens are different from the true greens of summer. Pinks range from soft to vivid, while yellows can be soft and buttery or sunny and daffodil bright.

The spring birth of lambs, bunnies, and chicks, along with the green blades of grass that pop up, refresh the spirit. Seasonal change, exciting and natural, varies from year to year, but it is always beautiful.

Spring is the only season I welcome earlier than the calendar indicates. Walking through winter's leftover snow, I collect crabapple branches to force into blooming, along with pussy willows and forsythia. I brush the snow from my purple crocus to help usher in the new season.

The papier-mâché creations for spring are a delightful way to bring the spirit and fresh colors into your home on a dark, chilly day in late winter or while waiting for a sign that the new season has arrived.

Spring hues have a vibrancy distinctive to the season. Flowers elicit a breath of fresh air. Vintage millinery once found on spring bonnets—silk violets and lilacs and luscious pastel satin ribbons, along with a sugary dusting—enhance many of the pieces.

In addition to rabbits, hares, and chicks, my home is filled with lots of eggs, the symbol of rebirth in nature and beautiful in their own right. This is the season when an egg can be any color.

Christopher the Heirloom Hare

Christopher is about 10" tall and his upright position, in chocolate mold lore, makes him a hare. Paws held high, he is a classic and would be very serious about his position in the meadow. He is a harbinger of spring and his texture and stiff posture remind me of wonderful stuffed antique bears sewn from mohair.

I paint my papier-mâché hares and rabbits in rich, deep, semi-sweet chocolate colors as well as softer hues.

In this project, Christopher is painted a rich vanilla color, frosted with crystal glitter, and then finished with a lovely yellow satin bow around his neck.

Instructions

Separate two-part mold; lay halves with interiors facing up on workspace. Spray mold with cooking spray; dab any excess with paper towel.

Shaping Figure

* Combine 2½ cups of dry papier-mâché and 1¾ cups of water in large bowl; mix thoroughly, removing all clumps. *Note: You have less than 30 minutes with this mixture before it becomes too dry.*

* Fill each side slightly above top edge of mold, pressing mixture firmly with your fingers to make certain crevices are completely filled in.

* *To set mold:* Place mold halves together, apply mold clips, and stand mold upright; let set about 1 hour and then remove mold clips.

* *To remove figure from mold:* Using paring knife, pry edges and gently remove half of the mold. There will be a little resistance. Lay in your hand, figure side up, and begin to repair, if necessary.

* Fill any large indentations with either a new, small batch of thick papier-mâché or small bits of the still-damp trimmings. If necessary, replace figure in mold and press together firmly with your hand for more extensive repairs; let set until firm, about 15 minutes. Turn mold over and repeat the repair process.

Materials

* 1½" satin ribbon: yellow (24")

* 10" metal rabbit mold

* Acrylic paint:
  black
  creamy white
  pale pink
  pink
  raw umber
  spring green
  yellow

* Cooking spray

* Dry papier-mâché: 2½ cups

* Fabric scissors

* Faux glaze medium: 2-ounce bottle

* Glitter: crystal

* Lint-free cloth

* Mold clips or rubber bands (2)

* Paintbrushes:
  1" craft
  No. 0 liner
  No. 5 round

* Paper towel

* Paring knife

* Vintage blossom

* White craft glue

ARTIST'S *notes*
All That Glitters

Pastel glitter, whether coarse, fine, or ultra-fine, makes a lovely finishing touch. Evenly coat your figure with diluted glue and then, very sparingly, sprinkle on pastel glitter. This is quite different than the sugary glitter as it is not translucent. A light sprinkling will allow your painting and mold details to shine through. Pink or red glitter on an ivory hare would create a delightful Valentine rabbit that can be tied with a pink or red moiré bow.

Trimming Figure

* Holding paring knife at 45-degree angle, trim seams formed from molding process, taking care when trimming ears. If the ears do break, fill ear section of mold from breaking point upwards with new 1 part water, 2 parts dry papier-mâché mixture. Place figure in mold and smooth line of repair with paring knife.

* Replace both halves of mold, press, and allow repair to set about 30 minutes before removing figure from mold. Figure should be damp but quite firm.

Drying Figure

* Place in 200-degree oven at least 3–5 hours; remove when dry and let cool.

Painting Figure

* Paint body creamy white using 1" craft brush; let air dry.

* *Using No. 5 round brush:* Paint nose and inside of ears pale pink; pink posy between his paws with a dab of yellow at the center; tiny blades of green grass around the base.

* *Using No. 0 liner brush:* Delicately draw black whiskers, mouth, and eyes as shown.

Applying Glaze

* Combine 2-ounce bottle of faux glaze medium, 2 ounces of water, and ½ teaspoon of raw umber paint in jar; mix well. Using lint-free cloth, gently rub figure with mixture, taking care around ears; let air dry 30 minutes.

Glittering Figure

* Mix ½ cup of craft glue and 1 tablespoon of water in a jar. Carefully and evenly coat rabbit with diluted glue mixture using 1" craft brush. Evenly sprinkle crystal glitter, covering all surfaces except the bottom; let dry completely 3–4 hours. *Note:* The details will be hidden by the glue and glitter until the glue dries.

Adding Finishing Touches

* Tie yellow ribbon around Christopher the Hare and into a bow, trimming ends with fabric scissors. Tuck vintage blossom behind bow.

Springtime Lamb

Several years ago I found this wonderful vintage chocolate mold, which I added to my growing collection. Figures made from lamb molds are sometimes lying down, sometimes standing.

His size makes him quite versatile. I sometimes place him next to village pieces, but often he lies alone on an antique book. I've completed his look with an old blue velvet ribbon trimmed to ¼" wide and embellished with a tiny bell.

Instructions

Separate two-part mold; lay halves with interiors facing up on workspace. Spray mold with cooking spray; dab any excess with paper towel.

Shaping Figure

★ *To make slurry:* Combine ½ cup of dry papier-mâché mix and ½ cup of water in large bowl; mix thoroughly, removing all clumps. Measure half of slurry mixture and spread evenly in half of mold. This will be quite wet. Cover sides of mold to just below top edge. Press firmly with your fingers to make certain crevices are completely filled in. Repeat with other side. Let set about 30 minutes.

★ *To make second layer:* Pour 1 cup of dry papier-mâché mix in large bowl and add ½ cup of water. Mix thoroughly, removing all clumps. This will be thicker than previous mixture. Spoon mixture into mold to just over top edge. Repeat with other half.

★ *To set mold:* Place mold halves together, applying mold clips; stand upright. Let set about 1 hour.

★ *To remove figure from mold:* Hold mold in your hand and gently loosen one side by prying with the paring knife. Go around all edges with the knife, prying gently until you can remove the top half. Using partially set papier-mâché mixture squeezed from the mold, repair any missing parts or details. If the figure requires major repair, fill area in with papier-mâché and press back into mold. Turn mold over and repeat with other half. Wait 5 minutes and check again. Repeat repairs if necessary.

Materials

- ¼" velvet ribbon: blue (8")
- 5" x 4" metal lamb mold
- Acrylic paint:
  black
  cream
  raw umber
  yellow-green
- Cooking spray
- Dry papier-mâché mix: 1½ cups
- Fabric scissors
- Faux glaze medium: 2-ounce bottle
- Glitter: crystal
- Hot-glue gun and glue sticks
- Lint-free cloth
- Mold clips or rubber bands: small (2)
- Paintbrushes:
  1" craft
  No. 0 round liner
  No. 5 round
  No. 10 flat
- Paper towel
- Paring knife
- Tiny bell
- White craft glue

Trimming Figure

★ Holding paring knife at 45-degree angle, trim seams formed from molding process. Figure should be damp but quite firm.

Drying Figure

★ Place figure in 200-degree oven 2–3 hours. Check bottom to see if figure is completely dry. If damp, wait overnight or return to oven until dry.

Painting Figure

★ *Using No. 10 flat brush:* Paint lamb cream.

★ *Using No. 5 round brush:* Paint nose, lining of ears, hooves, and eyes black.

★ *Using No. 0 round liner brush:* Paint tiny blades of grass yellow-green at the base, extending over the lamb's legs and hooves for a natural appearance.

Applying Glaze

★ Combine 2-ounce bottle of faux glaze, 2 ounces of water, and ¼ teaspoon of raw umber paint in small jar; mix well. Using lint-free cloth, gently rub figure with mixture; let air dry 30 minutes.

Glittering Figure

★ Dilute ¼ cup of white craft glue with 1 teaspoon water. Completely coat figure, except bottom, with diluted glue using 1" craft brush. Immediately cover in glitter.

Adding Finishing Touches

★ Measure ribbon by placing it around the lamb's neck and allowing an overlap of about ¼"; cut ribbon and then string on the bell. Place around the lamb's neck, turning one end under a bit to create a neat edge; hot glue in place.

ARTIST'S notes
Fit to be Tied

I love the timeworn look of old velvet, however, velvet ribbon is often too wide for a small figure. A bow would overwhelm and dominate the figure, so I trim wider ribbon to about a ¼" width. This can be placed on a figurine like a collar. My dog collection features collars of old velvet ribbon, the colors selected to enhance the dog's coat or to tie in with the current holiday season. Sentimental charms or small bells are strung onto the ribbon and secured with a dab of hot-glue.

Bunny Buddies Sharing a Basket

These whimsical bunnies seem to spring from the era when my treasured childhood memories began. More photographs were taken of my brothers and me during the Easter egg hunt than any other holiday. I can picture my own children Katie, Chris, and Susannah when they were small finding these buddies on Easter morning, either chocolate or as a delightful papier-mâché decoration.

Wonderfully nostalgic, the Bunny Buddies project is sentimental but definitely has an attitude. This piece represents friendship between its two companions all cozy in a basket.

A great quality of this piece is the sturdy ears. These two are solid little rabbits. The features are clear and will be reassuring to a new papier-mâché artist.

Materials

* 8" plastic buddies in a basket mold

* Acrylic paint:
  bright blue
  cream
  gold
  lavender
  pale aqua
  pale pink
  raw umber
  white

* Chenille pipe cleaners
  18" lavender
  18" pale blue

* Dry papier-mâché mix:
  4½ cups

* Faux glaze medium:
  2-ounce bottle

* Glitter: crystal

* Hot-glue gun and
  glue sticks

* Paintbrushes:
  1" craft
  No. 0 round liner
  No. 5 round

* Paring knife

* Piercing tool

* Rubber bands: small (2)

* Ultra-fine permanent
  marker: black

* White craft glue

Instructions

Separate two-part mold; lay halves with interiors facing up on workspace.

Shaping Figure

★ *To make slurry:* Combine 1 cup of dry papier-mâché mix and 1 cup of water in large bowl; mix thoroughly, removing all clumps. Measure half of slurry mixture and spread evenly in mold. This will be quite wet. Mixture should cover the mold, stopping short of the top. Repeat with remaining mixture and other half of mold. Let set about 1 hour.

★ *To make second layer:* Combine 3½ cups of dry papier-mâché mix and 1¾ cups of water in large bowl; mix thoroughly, removing all clumps. This will be thicker than the previous mixture. Working quickly, complete filling both sides of mold to a bit over the top, firmly pressing papier-mâché mixture into mold to fill in details.

★ *To set mold:* Place mold halves together, wrap with rubber bands, and then stand upright. Let set about 1 hour until firm.

★ *To remove figure from mold:* Lay mold in your hand and gently loosen one side by prying with edge of paring knife; remove top half. Using partially set papier-mâché that has been squeezed from the mold, repair any missing details. If figure requires major repairs, fill them in and press back into the mold; then turn mold over and repeat with the other half. Wait about 5 minutes and check. Repeat if necessary.

Experiment with Papier-Mâché

Papier-mâché can either be purchased pre-made at a crafts store or made by hand. I recommend a dry pre-made mix. There are several varieties; I use a snowy white, non-shrinking type. Don't worry if the manufacturer has added other ingredients, it is still papier-mâché. Experimenting is part of the fun and all varieties have their good qualities.

Trimming Figure

✴ Holding paring knife at 45-degree angle, trim seams formed from molding process. Rabbits should be firm but slightly damp.

✴ With piercing tool, puncture each side of basket for later insertion of chenille pipe cleaners.

Drying Figure

✴ Place figure in 200-degree oven 4–6 hours. Remove when dry and let cool.

Painting Figure

✴ *Using 1" craft brush:* Paint rabbits cream and basket gold.

✴ *Using No. 0 round liner brush:* Paint pale pink noses and white eyes with bright blue eye centers.

✴ *Using No. 5 round brush:* Paint white collar and pale aqua tie on taller rabbit and lavender ribbon on smaller rabbit.

Applying Glaze

✴ Combine ½ teaspoon of raw umber paint, 2-ounce bottle of faux glaze medium, and 2 ounces of water in small jar; mix well. Paint figure with glaze using 1" craft brush; let dry at least 2 hours. *Note:* Be sure to clean craft brush after use.

✴ Draw eyes, mouths, and whiskers and add black dots on eyes with black marker.

Glittering Figure

✴ Mix ½ cup of white craft glue with 1 tablespoon of water in a small jar. Completely coat rabbits with diluted glue using 1" craft brush.

✴ Evenly sprinkle crystal glitter over all surfaces of figure except the bottom; let air dry completely. The details of your work will be hidden by the glue and glitter until the glue dries clear.

Adding Finishing Touches

✴ Twist pipe cleaners together; dab hot glue in holes and insert chenille ends to secure.

ARTIST'S notes
Identifying Chenilles

Chenille comes in shades for all seasons. Spring has yummy pastels of blue, pink, and lavender. The brighter primary colors of summer include vivid yellows, bright pinks, and the fresh green of grass. For autumn there are rich golds and pumpkin oranges. Winter has reds both bright and faded along with wintry white and forest greens.

Vintage chenille is made of cotton or wool and is usually faded, which adds to its charm. The colors of new chenille do not change.

Any basket could use a handle made with chenille stems. A delicate papier-mâ-ché rabbit could have his ears trimmed right off and chenille could be looped to replace the ears. A piece of orange chenille could be shaped into a carrot and hot glued onto little rabbit paws. The colors and texture of chenille will inspire you to create your own embellishments.

There are several types of chenille. Chenille yarn has little form, much like wool yarn. This makes a wonderful trim glued around the edge of a cape on a papier-mâché St. Nick or used as an accent on a snowbaby.

The second type is chenille with a wire core, similar to a pipe cleaner. It is easy to shape into figures like a candy cane or heart, or twist it with a contrasting color to add interest.

The third type of chenille is bump chenille. This comes in wonderful colors and a variety of sizes. Bump chenille has a wire core and is classified by the length between the bumps (the thick sections of chenille).

Peter Rabbit

The wonderful personality of a little scamp of a rabbit, wearing his blue jacket, shines through on this piece. For many years I had a chalkware rabbit. Using silicone, I made a mold of this fellow and called him Peter.

From storybook lore, despite many maternal warnings, Peter catches his button on a wire fence and almost ends up in the soup pot of the farmer's wife. He does have a bit of an attitude with his long, floppy ears. He is a favorite creature in the springtime vegetable garden. His jacket is a pale bluish-green, his fur a soft cream, and of course, he definitely needs a pink twitchy nose. A satin ribbon completes his attire. I am sure he will join his more conservative sisters later, probably removing his bow and hiding it under a wheelbarrow.

Materials

* ⅝"-wide vintage satin ribbon: pale blue (24")
* 3"x 7" silicone floppy-eared rabbit mold
* Acrylic paint:
    cream
    metallic gold
    pink
    robin's-egg blue
    white
* Dry papier-mâché mix: 3 cups
* Fabric scissors
* Glitter: crystal
* Lint-free cloth
* Paintbrushes:
    1" craft
    No. 0 liner
    No. 5 round
* Paring knife
* Rubber band: small
* Ultra-fine permanent marker: black
* White craft glue

Instructions

Place silicone mold interior side up on work surface.

Shaping Figure

★ Mix 3 cups of dry papier-mâché mix with 1½ cups of water, removing all clumps. Press papier-mâché mixture firmly into both sides of mold to make certain all of the crevices are completely filled in.

★ *To set mold:* Stand mold up with open section on bottom and secure closed with rubber band. Make certain bottom is flat; if not, mix and add a bit more papier-mâché mixture through bottom part of mold. Let set about 45 minutes. Check bottom of figure; it should be damp but firm.

★ *To remove figure:* Hold mold on its side in your hand and gently loosen one side by prying with the paring knife. Go around all edges with the knife, prying gently until you feel a little give. Pry one half off and repair any missing parts that were not pressed completely into details. With such a pronounced nose, it is very likely that a part will be missing. If so, fill with extra wet mix and press into mold firmly. Repeat with other side.

Trimming Figure

✴ Holding paring knife at 45-degree angle, trim seams formed from molding process, taking care with the delicate ears. Remember, perfection is not necessary, and a bit of imperfection will give your piece character. Figure should be damp but quite firm.

Drying Figure

✴ Place figure in 200-degree oven about 5 hours. Return to the oven if the figure has any moisture.

Painting Figure

✴ *Using 1" craft brush:* Paint entire figure cream except the bottom.

✴ *Using No. 0 liner brush:* Paint nose and ear linings with a touch of pink.

✴ *Using No. 5 round brush:* Paint Peter Rabbit's coat robin's-egg blue and add three white buttons.

Applying Glaze

✴ Combine ½ cup of water and ¼ teaspoon of metallic gold paint in small jar; mix well. Using lint-free cloth, gently rub figure with mixture; let air dry several hours.

Adding Details

✴ Draw simple eyes and whiskers on each side of the rabbit's nose using the black marker.

Glittering Figure

✴ Using 1" craft brush, apply undiluted white craft glue to entire rabbit, except the bottom. Sprinkle heavily with crystal glitter; let dry at room temperature for several hours or overnight.

Adding Finishing Touches

✴ Tie floppy ribbon bow around the rabbit's neck and trim ends.

ARTIST'S notes
Which Paint Works Best

Available in a large variety of colors, acrylic paints are so convenient. I use them frequently, mixing almost each shade to match my vision for each of my papier-mâché creations. I apply acrylics with a light hand for their color, not their texture.

When I have a piece I want to paint ivory or white, I prefer latex paint applied heavily. This type of paint acts a bit like gesso, an artist's medium used to smooth canvas for painting. After the glaze or patina is applied, the latex-covered areas have an antique look, which is more pronounced than with acrylics. This aged patina is delightful and I use it often.

Yellow Chick's Fine Ride

This rabbit seems to be pulling a heavy load. His small size is not an obstacle, though the vehicle and its occupant could easily outweigh him. He is pulling his little friend and seems to be mustering all of his strength to do so.

The friend is a tiny chick and his vehicle is an egg. An egg, why not? The original occupant has already vacated it and the little chick has built himself a cart. He and his associate have added tiny wheels.

The original mold for this piece was a tiny, chipped, faded chalkware figure I unearthed in my attic a long time ago. Its origins are now forgotten but I made a silicone mold from the original. The figure is small and gives me a chance to use luscious spring colors such as pink and yellow.

Instructions

Separate two-part mold; lay halves with interiors facing up on workspace.

Shaping Figure

★ Pour 5 tablespoons of dry papier-mâché mix into large bowl and add 5 tablespoons of water. Mix thoroughly, removing all clumps. Working quickly, fill both sides to just over top edge. Firmly press papier-mâché mixture with fingers to make certain crevices are completely filled in. Place mold halves together, secure closed with rubber band, and stand upright with opening on bottom. Let set 30 minutes.

★ *To remove figure from mold:* Hold mold in your hand and gently loosen one side by prying with the paring knife. Go around all edges with the knife, prying gently until you can remove top half. Using partially set papier-mâché that has been squeezed from the mold, repair any missing parts or details. If the figure requires major repairs, fill them in and press the figure back into the mold. Turn mold over and repeat with other half. Wait about 5 minutes and check again. Repeat repairs if necessary.

Materials

- 3" x 2" silicone chick and egg mold

- Acrylic paint:
  black
  brown
  cream
  orange
  pink
  raw umber
  yellow
  yellow-green

- Dry papier-mâché mix: 5 tablespoons

- Faux glaze medium: 2-ounce bottle

- Glitter: crystal

- Lint-free cloth

- Paintbrushes:
  1" craft
  No. 0 round liner
  No. 5 round

- Paring knife

- Rubber band: small

- White craft glue

Trimming Figure

★ Holding paring knife at 45-degree angle, trim seams formed from molding process. Figure should be damp but quite firm.

Drying Figure

★ Place figure in 200-degree oven 2–3 hours. Check bottom to see if figure is completely dry. If damp, wait overnight or return to oven until dry.

Painting Figure

★ *Using No. 5 round brush:* Paint rabbit cream; chick yellow; egg cart pink.

★ *Using No. 0 round liner brush:* Paint nose and ear linings pink; all eyes and whiskers black; tiny beak orange; wooden parts and wheels brown; tiny blades of grass yellow-green on the base, extending a few over legs, wheels, and cart to create a natural appearance.

Applying Glaze

★ Combine 2-ounce bottle of faux glaze, 2 ounces of water, and ¼ teaspoon of raw umber paint in small jar; mix well. Using lint-free cloth, gently rub figure with mixture; let air dry 30 minutes.

Glittering Figure

★ Dilute ⅛ cup of white craft glue with ½ teaspoon of water. Coat figure with diluted glue using 1" craft brush. Immediately roll in glitter; let air dry at least 8 hours.

ARTIST'S notes
Storing Leftover Glaze

Many of the figures in this book don't require a great amount of glaze so inevitably you will have some left over. Store remaining glaze in a small jar with a lid. Label each jar with contents and save for another project. Sealed tightly, the glaze will last for months.

Two-Piece Egg with Painted Roses

Eggs are one of my favorite things—tiny broken eggshells of a hatched mourning dove under a tall pine tree; the pale blue-green of a robin's egg after the baby bird has vacated. On the window seat in my bedroom sits a tall glass cloche atop my collection of emus, ostrich, and goose eggs of all sizes and colors. I even have a large, deep emerald green emus egg.

This project is a fully decorated egg container with a soft lavender background and tiny sprigs of pale pink roses and spring green leaves. It's fun to fill with cellophane grass, chocolate candy, and small gifts. This piece is quite delicate and damp when removed from its mold, so be extra careful.

Materials

* 8"x 5½"x 6" plastic egg container mold

* Acrylic paint:
  lavender
  pale pink
  raw umber
  red
  white
  yellow
  yellow-green

* Cellophane grass

* Chenille chick

* Dry papier-mâché mix: 5 cups

* Faux glaze medium: 2-ounce bottle

* Filler: as desired

* Glitter: crystal

* Lint-free cloth

* Paintbrushes:
  1½" craft
  No. 0 round liner
  No. 5 round

* Paring knife

* Plastic tablespoon

* White craft glue

Instructions

Separate two-part mold; lay halves with interiors facing up on workspace.

Shaping Figure

* *To make slurry:* Combine 3 cups of dry papier-mâché mix and 3 cups of water in large bowl; mix thoroughly, removing all clumps.

* Measure half of wet papier-mâché mixture and spread evenly in the mold. This will be quite wet. Cover the bottom and sides of mold with slurry but don't be concerned if mixture slips down a bit. Press mixture with your fingers to make certain crevices are completely filled in. Repeat with bottom half of mold, smoothing exposed surfaces as best you can. The lower half of this mold is open at the base so leave it on your work surface with its bottom flat. This interior will be the base coat for the exposed part of your finished egg. Let set about 1 hour without joining halves.

* *To make second layer:* Pour 2 cups of dry papier-mâché mix into large bowl and add 1 cup of water. Mix thoroughly, removing all clumps. This will be thicker than previous mixture. Working quickly, reinforce egg with this thicker mixture. Spoon about half of the fresh mix into each half, filling just above top edge. This will be the top rim of the egg; don't join the two mold pieces. Smooth interior of each side with a plastic tablespoon. Let set at least 30 minutes, until completely dry.

45

* **To remove figure from mold:** Place lower half of mold bottom side up on work surface. Pull the mold up with one hand while pushing delicately down on damp but firm exposed papier-mâché with the other hand, flexing mold enough to release egg. Remove top half from mold by carefully inserting paring knife along entire edge at 1" intervals. This should loosen the figure a bit from the mold. Turn mold upside down and tap one end on a hard surface to release egg.

* Using partially set papier-mâché squeezed from the mold, repair any missing parts or details. If the figure requires major repairs, fill them in and press figure back into mold; repeat with other half. Wait about 5 minutes and check again. Repeat repairs if necessary.

Trimming Figure

* Using paring knife, carefully trim top edges. Allow egg to sit on work surface at least another hour before oven drying. Egg should be damp but quite firm before placing in oven.

Drying Figure

* Place figure in 200-degree oven 2–3 hours. Check bottom to see if figure is completely dry. If damp, wait overnight or return to oven until dry.

Painting Figure

* Paint entire egg lavender using 1½" craft brush; let dry. Following embossing pattern on egg, apply touch of pale pink on several roses.

* *Using No. 5 round brush:* Tip your brush lightly in pink paint and immediately dip deeper into white paint; apply to 2–3 roses at a time; let dry. Repeat this technique using tip of brush dipped in red paint and then deeper into white to paint additional roses. *Note:* Don't rinse your brush in between flowers—roses have more depth when painted more than one color.

* *Using No. 0 round liner brush:* Add yellow-green stems and leaves and a few yellow centers; let dry.

Applying Glaze

* Combine 2-ounce bottle of faux glaze medium, 2 ounces of lukewarm water, and ¼ teaspoon of raw umber paint in small jar; mix well. Using lint-free cloth, gently rub figure with mixture; let air dry 30 minutes.

Glittering Figure

* Apply white craft glue over entire figure except interior and bottom of egg using 1½" craft brush. Heavily sprinkle with crystal glitter; let air dry at least 5 hours.

Adding Finishing Touches

* Fill egg with desired materials such as cellophane grass, treats, and small treasures. If desired, add a few chenille chicks in yellow and pink or a trio of candy eggs.

Newly Hatched Chick in Egg

The mold used for this project is an opaque plastic candy mold. This figure is pure simplicity—the beginning of life with a small yellow chick sitting serenely in his half egg all by himself.

When I was about seven, I held a little newborn chick during a photo shoot for the *Sunday Parade* magazine. Red moiré ribbon was tied in a bow around my ponytail, which had been curled overnight with strips of cotton rags. The dress I wore was bright red and white dotted Swiss with puffy sleeves and a full skirt. Freshly starched, the dress had a bow tied in the back. I was not supposed to move and neither was my co-star, a boy named Stuart who was wearing a red plaid wool jacket. Stuart was posed leaning over a chair and looking at his Easter basket. Somehow they placed a minutes-old chick, his feathers barely dried, in our hands and the camera clicked. The fuzzy new chick was gone just as quickly as he arrived. This little figure reminds me of that day.

Materials

* 2½"-square plastic chick in egg candy mold

* Acrylic paint:
    gloss white
    metallic gold
    orange
    yellow

* Cooking spray

* Dry papier-mâché mix: ¾ cup

* Faux glaze medium: 2-ounce bottle

* Glitter: crystal

* Lint-free cloth

* Paper towel

* Paintbrushes:
    No. 0 round liner
    No. 5 round

* Paring knife

* Rubber band: small

* Ultra-fine permanent marker: black

* White craft glue

Instructions

Separate two-part mold; lay halves with interiors facing up on workspace. Spray mold with cooking spray; dab any excess with paper towel.

Shaping Figure

★ *To make slurry:* Combine ¼ cup of dry papier-mâché mix and ¼ cup of water in large bowl; mix thoroughly.

★ Measure half of slurry mixture and spread evenly in mold. This will be quite wet. The mixture should not go all the way to the top so leave about ⅛" of the mold free of mixture. (The two mold parts need to join together so we will not fill to the top until the last filling.) Press firmly with fingers so crevices are completely filled in. Repeat with other half of mold. Let mold set on its side about 30 minutes.

★ *To make second layer:* Pour ½ cup of dry papier-mâché mix into large bowl and add ¼ cup of water. Mix thoroughly, removing all clumps. This will be thicker than the previous mixture.

* Working quickly, completely fill both sides a bit over top edge of mold with papier-mâché mixture; press mixture firmly with fingers to fill in details.

* *To set mold:* Place mold halves together. Secure closed with rubber band and then lay mold on its side; let set about 45 minutes.

* *To remove figure from mold:* Hold mold in your hand and gently loosen one side by prying with the paring knife. Go around all edges with the knife, prying gently until you can remove top half. Using partially set papier-mâché that has been squeezed from the mold, repair any missing parts or details. If the figure requires major repairs, fill them in and press back into the mold. Turn mold over and repeat with other half. Wait 5 minutes and check again. Repeat repairs if necessary.

Trimming Figure

* Holding paring knife at 45-degree angle, trim seams formed from molding process. Figure should be damp but quite firm.

Drying Figure

* Place figure in 200-degree oven 2–3 hours. Check bottom to see if figure is completely dry. If still damp, wait overnight or return to oven until dry.

Painting Figure

* *Using No. 5 round brush:* Paint egg gloss white; paint chick yellow.

* *Using No. 0 round liner brush:* Paint beak orange; let dry thoroughly. Using marker, draw chick's eyes.

Applying Glaze

* Combine 2-ounce bottle of faux glaze medium, 2 ounces of water, and ½ teaspoon of metallic gold paint in small jar; mix well. Using lint-free cloth, gently rub figure with mixture; let air dry 30 minutes.

Glittering Figure

* Mix ¼ cup of white craft glue with 1 teaspoon of water and paint mixture everywhere except bottom of egg using No. 5 round brush. Immediately roll figure in crystal glitter. Let air dry 8 hours.

ARTIST'S notes
Cleaning Plastic Molds

I sometimes use mild detergent as a release agent when working with plastic molds. This is not a necessity but it does facilitate figure removal. Clean mold with mild detergent and water immediately following use to ensure a longer life of the mold. This mold can be used dozens of times.

Old-Fashioned Peek-a-Boo Egg

This lovely egg is created from a purchased fiber egg, molded like the old-fashioned cardboard Santa figures and bunnies from the past. We need no dry papier-mâché mix for this beautiful egg.

The peek-a-boo egg brings so many memories to mind. When my three children were very young, they were enchanted by sugared eggs. Each spring, the Easter Bunny would bring such a treasure, sometimes via Mom and sometimes via our thoughtful Great Aunt Nancy.

I have a small collection of these sugared beauties from the past. Miraculously, they have survived the mice that have crept into the attic to escape winter. My all-time favorite sugar egg was bought at an estate sale. The original coloring has mellowed into a soft yellow and the icing around the opening is a faded pale green. The tiny chenille chicks and grassy scene inside is simply magical.

For this nostalgic project, I purchased the egg form, a pressed-cardboard piece like the ones from the past, and added my own personal touches.

Materials

* 2"-wide ribbon: cream with pale rose-colored edges (40")
* 8" hollow fiber kraft egg
* Acrylic paint: pale green
* Cardboard box: 6" square
* Cardboard scrap: about 5" square
* Cellophane grass: pink
* Chenille chick: pink
* Craft knife
* Drinking glass with 3¼"-diameter opening
* Glitter: crystal
* Hot-glue gun and glue sticks
* Latex semi-gloss paint: white
* Paintbrushes:
  1" craft
  No. 5 round
* Paper rabbit image
* Pastel eggs: small (3)
* Pencil
* Tube of caulking
* Vintage millinery flowers (4)
* White craft glue

Instructions

Trace the mouth of the drinking glass on the narrow end of the kraft egg using a pencil. Using a craft knife, cut out circle to create the opening of the egg.

Shaping Figure

★ Soak new opening in water about 3 minutes. While damp, use fingers to smooth fibers and edges for easier painting; let dry.

★ Using craft knife, cut out a circle from cardboard square, about ¼" larger than bottom opening in egg. This circle will eventually be placed inside the egg.

Painting Figure

★ Paint circle white; let dry and apply a second coat. Paint egg inside and out white. This will act a bit like gesso and smooth the rough cardboard. When you paint the inside, fibers will flake in your brush. This is fine, just make certain your craft brush is completely free of these fibers when you paint the outside; let dry. Repeat with a second coat. *Note:* If the brown of the fiber egg still shows through the paint, apply another coat of paint.

51

* Paint outside of egg pale green; let dry. Hot glue cardboard circle inside egg. (The circle is a support for your embellishments in the interior of your egg.)

* Using craft knife, snip tube of caulking, giving it an opening of about ¼". Squeeze a line around the entire outside opening of the egg as a base coat. Hold caulking tube on the surface of the egg, at the opening. Squeeze while pulling tube away from opening in an irregular pattern, much like icicles. Release pressure and pull tube away. Repeat all around opening. Smooth a bit with fingers; let dry completely. Paint caulking white using No. 5 round brush; let dry.

Glittering Figure

* Dilute ¼ cup of white craft glue with 1 teaspoon of water. Paint glue on entire exterior of egg using 1" craft brush. Sprinkle with glitter; let dry 2–4 hours.

Adding Finishing Touches

* Hot glue cellophane grass in egg. *Note:* This can be tricky as grass melts so work slowly and just try to anchor grass a bit.

* Loosely arrange image of rabbit, millinery flowers, pink chick, and small pastel eggs on cellophane grass on bottom of egg. Wrap ribbon around the egg and tie a bow on top.

Rabbit Pulling Egg Carriage

I have made this figure in different sizes. The tiny one is fun and so Lilliputian—he can only manage a couple of jelly beans in his egg.

The next size has an egg cart that could probably hold about four pigeon eggs. I have replaced the old metal chocolate mold I had originally used with a more durable plastic chocolate mold. I have an advantage over a chocolatier and chalkware maker because I can easily remove the inside of a rabbit's basket or create a hollow egg cart.

Materials

* 6" x 5" rabbit pulling egg wagon plastic mold

* Acrylic paint:
    cream
    green
    lavender
    light brown
    pale pink
    raw umber

* Cellophane grass: pink

* Chenille chick

* Dry papier-mâché mix: 2 cups

* Faux glaze medium: 2-ounce bottle

* Foil-covered eggs (5)

* Glitter: crystal

* Lint-free cloth

* Mold clips or rubber bands: small (2)

* Paintbrushes:
    1" craft
    No. 0 round liner
    No. 5 round
    No. 10 flat

* Paring knife

* Plastic tablespoon

* Ultra-fine permanent marker: black

* White craft glue

Instructions

Separate two-part mold; lay halves with interiors facing up on workspace.

Shaping Figure

✱ To make slurry: Combine 1 cup of dry papier-mâché mix and 1 cup of water in large bowl; mix thoroughly, removing all clumps. Measure half of slurry mixture and spread evenly in mold. This slurry will be quite wet. Spread mixture to just below top edge of mold. Press firmly with fingers to make certain crevices are completely filled in. Egg is to be a thick shell so smooth with plastic tablespoon. Repeat with other side of mold; let set about 1 hour.

✱ To make second layer: Pour 1 cup of dry papier-mâché mix into large bowl and add ½ cup of water. Mix thoroughly, removing all clumps. This will be thicker than the previous mixture. Working quickly, completely fill both sides of rabbit but leave cavity in egg accessible through mold opening. Press papier-mâché mixture firmly to fill details. Smooth interior of egg with plastic tablespoon.

✱ Place mold halves together, apply mold clips, and stand upright. Let set about 1 hour.

* *To remove figure from mold:* Hold mold in your hand and gently loosen one side by prying with paring knife. Go around all edges with paring knife, prying gently until you can remove top half. Using partially set papier-mâché mixture squeezed from mold, repair any missing parts or details. If the figure requires major repairs, fill in with papier-mâché and press figure back into mold. Turn mold over and repeat with other half. Wait about 5 minutes and check again. Repeat repairs if necessary.

Trimming Figure

* Holding paring knife at 45-degree angle, trim seams formed from molding process. Figure should be damp but quite firm. With your fingers and knife, smooth interior of egg.

Drying Figure

* Place figure in 200-degree oven 6–8 hours. Check bottom to see if figure is completely dry. If damp, wait overnight or return to oven until dry.

Painting Figure

* *Using No. 10 flat brush:* Paint entire rabbit cream; paint egg lavender.

* *Using No. 0 round liner brush:* Paint cart handle and wheels light brown; add pale pink nose and ear linings.

* *Using No. 5 round brush:* Paint green grass blades all around the figure, including some over the wheels, egg, and rabbit to mimick naturally growing grass.

Applying Glaze

* Combine 2-ounce bottle of faux glaze medium, 2 ounces of water, and ½ teaspoon of raw umber paint in small jar; mix well. Using lint-free cloth, gently rub figure with mixture; let air dry about 2 hours. Draw eyes and whiskers using black marker.

Glittering Figure

* Dilute ½ cup of white craft glue with 2 teaspoons of water. Paint figure with diluted glue everywhere using 1" craft brush, except bottom of rabbit. Immediately roll in crystal glitter; let air dry at least 6 hours.

Adding Finishing Touches

* Fill egg loosely with cellophane grass, pulling some strands over the top. Casually arrange chenille chick and foil eggs in grass.

Chapter 3

Summer

During my childhood, I made some of the best mud pies in Denver, Colorado. Sifted and stirred into my grandmother's 3" blue graniteware bowl, I rolled out my mud dough with a small blue-handled rolling pin and then sun baked it in tiny vintage brownie pans. Each pie was then decorated with berries or tiny flowers I picked from my mother's garden. These were my earliest art projects. I had no manual or how-to book; it was all about experience and proportion, just like papier-mâché.

When my three children were small, we spent every sunny day at the pool. I added nasturtiums and violets to our salads, and we enjoyed fresh iced tea with homegrown mint and hosting low-profit lemonade stands. Summer has an attitude, and I try to capture the feeling of these special days in each of my summertime pieces.

These days, projects need to be very special to entice me and my grandbaby, Jack, to leave the beach.

Throughout this chapter I've selected soft paint colors for the papier-mâché figures. Pure white is always a dreamy background, while the pale peach of a summer rose in full bloom and the translucent pink of a conch stir delicious summer images. Weddings, the family dog lazing around on a hot day, the constant companion of children, vintage, softly-colored flowers, and of course, the beach, are all joyful summertime memories. Let your memories inspire you to create your own heirloom projects.

Basket of Flowers

During the 1800s, early chalkware pieces were made by itinerant peddlers as an alternative to the more expensive Staffordshire figurines. A century later, carnivals offered this plaster of Paris figure. Each piece was delicate and many were hollow, which is perhaps why few have survived. Artists today make chalkware, most of it solid, out of the same chocolate molds I first used to create my papier-mâché projects.

I strive for a nostalgic look, and I love this little flower basket in papier-mâché, inspired by the vintage hollow chalkware.

Instructions

Separate two-part mold; lay halves with interiors facing up on workspace.

Shaping Figure

* *To make slurry:* Combine ⅛ cup of dry papier-mâché mix and ⅛ cup of water in small bowl; mix thoroughly.

* Measure 1 tablespoon of slurry and spread evenly into one side of mold. This will be quite wet. Pull mixture up sides of mold but not quite to the top. Press firmly with your fingers to make certain crevices are completely filled in. Repeat with 1 tablespoon of mixture on other side of mold. Let set about 1 hour.

* *To make second layer:* Combine ½ cup of dry papier-mâché mix and ¼ cup of water into large bowl; mix thoroughly, removing all clumps. This will be thicker than the previous mixture.

* Working quickly, completely fill both sides just over top edge of mold; press papier-mâché mixture with fingers to fill in mold's details.

* Place mold halves together; secure closed with rubber bands and lay mold on its side. Let set about 1 hour.

* *To remove figure from mold:* Hold mold in your hand; gently loosen one side by prying it apart using paring knife. Still holding mold, remove top half. Taking partially set papier-mâché squeezed from the mold, repair any parts or details that were missed in the second layer using your fingers and paring knife. If figure requires major repairs, fill in with papier-mâché mixture and press back into mold. Turn mold over and repeat with other half. Wait about 5 minutes and check again. Repeat if necessary.

Materials

* 3" x 4½" plastic flower basket mold

* Acrylic paint:
    bright blue
    golden brown
    green
    pink
    raw umber
    red
    white
    yellow

* Dry papier-mâché mix: ⅝ cup

* Faux glaze medium: 2-ounce bottle

* Glitter: crystal

* Lint-free cloth

* Paintbrushes:
    1" craft
    No. 5 round

* Paring knife

* Rubber bands: small (2)

* White craft glue

Trimming Figure

★ Holding paring knife at 45-degree angle, trim seams formed from molding process. Figure should be damp but quite firm.

Drying Figure

★ Place figure in 200-degree oven 2–3 hours. Check bottom to see if figure is completely dry. If damp, return to oven until dry or air dry overnight.

Painting Figure

★ *Using No. 5 round brush:* Paint flower basket and handle golden brown; white daisies with yellow centers; tiny bright blue forget-me-nots with yellow centers on both sides; add green leaves to all flowers. Dip brush in pink paint and then just the tip in white paint to make roses; follow by dipping brush in red paint and then tip in white paint. Don't rinse your brush until you have finished all of the roses. Several shades of reds and pinks will be created on each rose petal by alternately dipping brush in white and red. This makes a subtle, realistically colored rose.

Applying Glaze

★ Combine 2-ounce bottle of faux glaze, 2 ounces of water, and ¼ teaspoon of raw umber paint in small jar; mix well. Using lint-free cloth, gently rub figure with mixture; let air dry 30 minutes.

Glittering Figure

★ Dilute ⅛ cup of white craft glue with ⅛ teaspoon of water and apply with 1" craft brush to entire piece. Roll piece in glitter; let dry.

ARTIST'S notes
Hints on Painting

Tiny crevices form as papier-mâché dries, giving the pieces an irregular surface. Details on papier-mâché are not exact and present a forgiving surface for painting.

To me, this is part of the charm of my work. Paper absorbs moisture quickly so I keep my paintbrush quite wet. I prefer subtlety and don't want to overload the piece with paint, allowing the natural qualities of the paper to be apparent, never disguised. Cream paint is almost always on my work table to soften even the most delicate pastels. When painting flowers, I don't rinse my brush until I've finished with that particular color palette.

Delicate White Stork

Midsummer's Day is June 21, the summer solstice and the longest day of the year. In pagan Europe, this is a traditional day for celebrations. Storks, with their long wingspan, are highly migratory, leaving Europe in the fall for the warmer climes of Africa. They avoid flying over water and will travel over Gibraltar to avoid the Mediterranean Sea. After the journey, the white bird returns to central and northern Europe just nine months after Midsummer's Day. Storks don't migrate together but often return to the same spot year after year to nest with the same partner.

Fidelity, fertility, prosperity, familial responsibility—no wonder Europeans encourage storks to build their ungainly nests atop their chimneys!

This little stork is an exquisite, delicate figure. The original metal mold used to make it is long gone so I use a plastic chocolate mold created from the original.

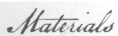

Materials

* 5" metal stork mold
* Acrylic paint:
  green
  raw umber
  terra cotta
* Dry papier-mâché mix:
  ½ cup
* Fabric scissors
* Faux glaze medium:
  2-ounce bottle
* Glitter: crystal
* Latex paint: white
* Lint-free cloth
* Paintbrushes:
  1" craft
  No. 3 round
  No. 5 round
* Paring knife
* Ribbon: white (12")
* Rubber band: small
* Ultra-fine permanent marker: black
* Vintage millinery
* White craft glue

Instructions

Separate two-part mold; lay halves with interiors facing up on workspace.

Shaping Figure

* *To make slurry:* Combine ¼ cup of dry papier-mâché mix and ¼ cup of water in small bowl; mix thoroughly, removing all clumps. Apply thin layer of mixture onto one side of mold, covering all details and pulling mixture up, almost to top edge. Repeat on other side. Be certain to carefully fill the long neck and the stork's back to just under the top edge of the mold. Let set about 20 minutes, until slightly firm.

* *To make second layer:* Mix ⅛ cup of water and ¼ cup of dry papier-mâché mix in small bowl, removing all clumps. Completely fill mold with mixture, filling just over top edges. Press two sides of mold together, stand mold upright, and secure closed with rubber band if necessary. Let set until bottom feels damp but firm, about 30 minutes.

* *To remove figure from mold:* Remove rubber band and lay mold on its side in your hand; gently pry using paring knife until one half pulls free of the mold. Repair any missing parts or defects with damp papier-mâché mixture that has squeezed out of mold. Apply a small amount of pressure and place mold on top of repairs for about 5 minutes. Repeat on other side.

Trimming Figure

* Holding paring knife at 45-degree angle, trim seams formed from molding process. Figure should be damp but quite firm.

* The stork's neck is thin and delicate so be gentle and patient. I always cut a space between his neck and body, allowing an opening for the ribbon.

Drying Figure

* Place figure in 200-degree oven 2–4 hours, or until dry.

Painting Figure

* *Using No. 5 round brush:* Paint body with a thick coat of white latex paint.

* *Using No. 3 round brush:* Paint legs and beak terra cotta and fine blades of grass green.

Applying Glaze

* Combine ½ of 2-ounce bottle of faux glaze medium, 1 ounce of water, and ¼ teaspoon of raw umber paint in small bowl; mix well. Using lint-free cloth, gently rub stork with mixture, highlighting feathers and other details; let dry completely. *Note:* The figure is paper and the water-based glaze makes him very delicate, so handle carefully.

* Draw eyes with black marker.

Glittering Figure

* Combine 2 teaspoons of white craft glue and 1–2 drops of water; brush on figure using 1" craft brush. Immediately sprinkle with glitter.

Adding Finishing Touches

* If your ribbon is wider than ¼", cut along length to create ¼" width. Gently weave half of ribbon through neck and body and then tie a small, droopy bow. Trim ends evenly at an angle, leaving as much length as possible. Tuck vintage millinery behind bow.

Susannah Elizabeth

When I first saw this figure, it was years ago. She was a sweet confection standing in the window of the most magical chocolate shop I had ever seen. I knew the mold existed because this chocolate maker had an extensive collection of vintage metal molds, many displayed in his storefront, which was filled with chocolate figures for all seasons and occasions.

Years later I saw the old metal mold itself for sale in an antiques store. I still loved her and wished to make her in papier-mâché. I pictured her in a white dress ready to walk to the seashore.

This figure gives me the opportunity to sprinkle a bit of magical sand at her feet. The mold has shoes, but for summer she is barefoot, a simple change made with a cut using a paring knife. A fun accent for this sweet summer girl is a mold of tiny seashells.

Instructions

Separate two-part mold; lay halves with interiors facing up on workspace. Spray mold with cooking spray; dab any excess with paper towel.

Shaping Figure

★ *To make slurry:* Combine ¼ cup of dry papier-mâché mix and ¼ cup of water in small bowl; mix thoroughly, removing all clumps. Pour papier-mâché mixture into mold and press thoroughly, filling just short of top edge; let set 30 minutes. If there is excess water after 10 minutes, dab with paper towel.

★ *To make second layer:* Mix ½ cup of dry papier-mâché mix with ¼ cup of water and fill mold just over top edge. Stand mold upright and secure closed with mold clips; let set 30 minutes.

Trimming Figure

★ Gently pry mold in several spots using paring knife. When figure feels like it is separating from the mold, you are ready for the next step.

★ Remove top half of mold and begin repairing figure with paring knife. It is helpful to have figure lying in your hand, still supported by the back half of the metal mold. Any missing features can be fixed with the little bits and pieces of partially set mix on your work surface.

Materials

- 2¼" x 5¾" metal Victorian girl mold
- Acrylic paint:
  light peach
  pale blue
  red
  silver
  white
  yellow
- Cooking spray
- Dry papier-mâché mix: ¾ cup
- Faux glaze medium: 1 ounce
- Glitter:
  ultra-fine pastel aqua
  ultra-fine pastel blue
- Lint-free cloth
- Mold clips or rubber band (2)
- Paintbrushes:
  No. 0 round liner
  No. 5 round
- Paper towel
- Paring knife
- Ultra-fine permanent marker: black
- White craft glue

* When repairing the doll, check the details in the mold and try to match them on the papier-mâché piece. If it is too difficult, remove the doll from the figure with the paring knife and add a crease or two for dress detail.

* To make this girl ready for the beach, we need to remove her shoes. Gently press the outsides of the line, forming her shoes back into the figure using your paring knife and fingers.

* Replace top of mold and place figure face down in your hand. Repeat any repairs needed on the back of the figure using leftover pieces of papier-mâché.

* Remove mold from figure. Re-check front to make certain she is still barefoot. (The mold may have re-imprinted her shoes.) With the figure lying in your hand, use the flat blade of the paring knife to apply pressure to the lower ¼" edge of her dress to create a pinafore look. Holding paring knife at 45-degree angle, trim seams formed from molding process. Figure should be damp but quite firm.

Drying Figure
* Place figure in 200-degree oven 2–4 hours. Set on the work surface overnight to continue drying or return to oven if necessary.

Painting Figure
* *Using No. 5 round brush:* Paint bare feet, legs, and face light peach; doll face and arms light peach; hair yellow and draw simple pigtails on her doll; entire dress white, extending into area below bottom hem of pinafore; base at her feet white.

* *Using No. 0 round liner brush:* Add pale blue highlights as shown on pictured figure. These will be tiny lines on her collar, stripes on the dress beneath her pinafore, and the edging on her sleeves; these dress-making details add to her charm. Paint empire waist on her pinafore and doll's tiny dress pale blue. Paint a red mouth on the girl and her doll and add red buttons down her dress. Her rosy cheeks are formed using this same liner brush dipped in red paint and then rinsed. Paint a watercolor pink on her cheeks by mixing red and white paints.

Applying Glaze
* Combine 1 ounce of faux glaze medium, ¼ teaspoon of silver paint, and 2 tablespoons of water in small bowl; mix well. Using lint-free cloth, gently rub figure with mixture; let dry completely. Draw eyes and eyebrows on girl with marker. Add dots for her doll's eyes.

Glittering Figure
* *Using No. 0 round liner brush*: Apply white craft glue to the stripes on the collar and portion of dress extending beyond the pinafore. Add a blue line defining the empire waist of the pinafore, sleeve detailing, and the doll's blue dress. Sprinkle all glue areas with pastel blue glitter.

* Paint undiluted white craft glue on base all around feet and sprinkle heavily with aqua glitter; let dry.

Materials

* 24-cavity plastic ocean creatures sheet

* Acrylic paint: white

* Cookie sheet

* Dry papier-mâché mix: ⅜ cup

* Glitter:
  diamond dust crystal
  ultra-fine pink
  ultra-fine bright blue

* Paintbrush: No. 5 round

* Paring knife

* Wax paper

* White craft glue

Seashells
Instructions

Lay mold of seashells flat, facing up on workspace.

Shaping Seashells

★ Mix ⅛ cup of water with ⅛ cup of firmly packed dry papier-mâché mix until smooth. Fill each cavity with wet mixture. Carefully turn mold over and place face down on your work surface.

★ After 30 minutes the seashells will be ready to remove from mold. If you pull mold up, away from work surface and there is no resistance, the pieces are done. If there is still resistance, let sit for 5–10 minutes.

★ Using a twisting motion much like removing ice from a plastic ice cube tray, hold each end of the mold and twist about 2" above your work surface. Most pieces will pop out, but a few may need to be coaxed out by prying with the paring knife. Repair any missing parts with leftover bits and those still clinging on the mold. Replace any seashells back into mold to regain shape.

Trimming Seashells

★ Trim edges and any papier-mâché that is not a part of a seashell using paring knife.

Drying Seashells

★ Dry shells on a cookie sheet in 150- to 200-degree oven about 1 hour.

Painting Seashells

★ Paint all shells white on both sides.

Glittering Seashells

★ Paint stripes on seashells with undiluted white craft glue. Sprinkle periwinkles with bright blue glitter over wax paper. Sparsely sprinkle pink glitter on sea biscuit and crystal glitter thickly on sand dollar. Use leftover and combined glitters on the wax paper and apply these to the moon snails.

Jack Christopher the Victorian Boy

Jack Christopher is formed from an old tin mold. He has a wide-brimmed hat and a toy horse at his feet. He is a wonderful companion for the Victorian girl; in fact, he looks like he might be her brother. I have made variations of Jack and his sister for all four seasons.

For this summer project, I've made Jack Christopher a sun-bleached blond. To make him more fun, and I'm certain a Victorian boy would be all about fun, I've removed the shoes from the figure using my paring knife. He needs sandy glitter on his bare feet.

Having fun with the variety of glitter hues available, I chose ultra-fine aqua for the sand and a brighter blue metallic glitter for the accents.

Instructions

Separate two-part mold; lay halves with interiors facing up on workspace. Lightly coat interior with dishwashing liquid; dab any excess with paper towel.

Shaping Figure

* *To make slurry:* Combine ½ cup of dry papier-mâché mix and ½ cup of water in large bowl; mix thoroughly, removing all clumps. Pour ½ of mixture into each side of mold. Spread into entire mold, filling just short of top edge. Make certain mixture sinks into mold details; let set about 30 minutes. If tiny pools of water remain after 10 minutes, lightly dab moisture with paper towel.

* *To make second layer:* Mix ½ cup of dry papier-mâché mix with ¼ cup of water. Mix well and finish filling mold, just over edges so no gaps are left in the sides of your figure when mold is secured. Close mold, stand upright, and, if necessary, apply mold clips. Let set 30 minutes.

* *To remove figure from mold:* Lay mold on its back in your hand. Gently pry the edges with paring knife. When you feel less resistance, remove the top half with paring knife.

* Leaving the figure in the back half of your mold for support, make any repairs using papier-mâché squeezed from the closed mold. Take partially set mix and, pressing on the figure, shape to fit repair. Place mold over figure, and then press. Remove and repeat as needed. Don't be concerned about the details of the figure's feet.

Materials

* 2¼" x 6" metal Victorian boy mold

* Acrylic paint:
  bright white
  brown
  golden brown
  light peach
  navy blue
  red
  rose
  silver metallic
  yellow

* Dishwashing liquid

* Dry papier-mâché mix: 1 cup

* Glitter:
  crystal
  metallic bright blue
  ultra-fine aqua

* Lint-free cloth

* Mold clips or rubber bands: small (2)

* Paintbrushes:
  1" craft
  No. 0 round liner
  No. 5 round

* Paper towel

* Paring knife

* Ultra-fine permanent marker: black

* White craft glue

My favorite method for painting cheeks is to dip the tip of a fine brush in red paint, then wash most of the paint off in water and make a watercolor wash of pink. I make strokes on the side of my hand until it is light pink and then paint a rosy glow on the cheeks.

✶ Replace front of mold to use as support, turn over, and repeat with any repairs after removing back of mold.

✶ After the back of the figure looks complete, replace back half of metal mold and place figure face upwards in your hand. (This is to support the wet figure.) Using paring knife and your fingers, press outline of shoes back into damp papier-mâché figure.

Trimming Figure

✶ Holding paring knife at a 45-degree angle, trim seams formed from molding process. Figure should be damp but quite firm.

Drying Figure

✶ Place figure in 200-degree oven 2–4 hours, until completely dry.

Painting Figure

✶ *Using No. 5 round brush:* Paint hat yellow; shirt white; pants navy blue; bare legs, feet, hands, and face light peach; hair golden brown; base white.

✶ *Using No. 0 round liner brush:* Trim outfit as shown in photo with tiny navy blue stripes on the collar and a brown belt; paint stick brown; smiling mouth red; cheeks rose.

Glazing Figure

✶ Mix ¼ teaspoon of silver metallic paint with 2 tablespoons of water in small paper cup. Using lint-free cloth, rub glaze over entire figure; let air dry 30 minutes. When completely dry, draw eyes and eyebrows with marker.

Glittering Figure

✶ Dilute white craft glue by adding ¼ teaspoon of water to 1 tablespoon of glue. Apply to entire figure using 1" craft brush. Sparsely sprinkle shirt and pants with bright blue glitter. While still damp, sprinkle lightly with a tiny bit of crystal glitter; let dry.

✶ Apply undiluted glue using No. 5 round brush on collar, hat rim, and base; sprinkle heavily with aqua glitter.

Four Bunnies with Flower Container

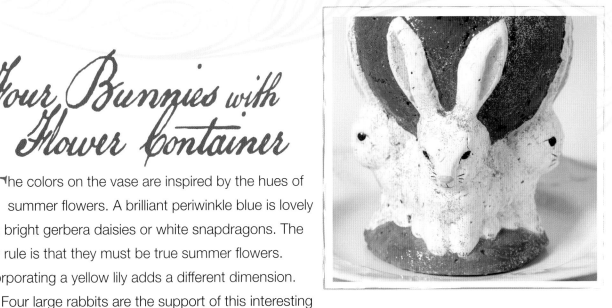

The colors on the vase are inspired by the hues of summer flowers. A brilliant periwinkle blue is lovely with bright gerbera daisies or white snapdragons. The only rule is that they must be true summer flowers. Incorporating a yellow lily adds a different dimension.

Four large rabbits are the support of this interesting shape. I insert a drinking glass as my vase because, after all, the figure is paper. When creating summer projects, I prefer a soft, shimmering glitter.

Instructions

Open mold and lay on work surface, open side up.

Shaping Figure

✷ Combine 2½ cups of water and 4 cups of papier-mâché mix in large bowl; mix thoroughly, removing all clumps. Fill mold halves with wet papier-mâché mixture. This piece is hollow but we need walls for support and details. Let set about 20 minutes, until firm enough to cling to sides of mold. With your fingers and a plastic spoon, pull mixture up sides of mold to the top. After a few minutes, when mixture has become partially firm, press damp papier-mâché upwards toward the top again.

✷ Smooth interior seams with your fingers to make certain sides fuse together.

Stand in an upright position by jamming mold upright into cardboard box a bit smaller than the mold; let set until firm, about 30 minutes. Smooth interior with plastic spoon. If mixture has shifted downwards and there are gaps at the top of the figure, make another batch of wet papier-mâché using 1 part water, 2 parts dry papier-mâché mix and add to top. This will not affect your piece as mixture can be added anytime before or after the piece has dried.

✷ Gently pop the mold halves away from figure by inserting paring knife into sides of mold. Repair any details not captured in the original casting with leftover wet papier-mâché scraps. Place back into mold briefly for shaping or sculpt repairs with paring knife, if necessary.

Materials

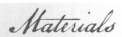

* 5" x 7" plastic four bunnies mold

* Acrylic paint:
    bright emerald green
    periwinkle blue
    pink
    raw umber
    white

* Cardboard box for supporting mold (slightly smaller than mold bottom)

* Drinking glass or jar

* Dry papier-mâché mix: 4 cups

* Faux glaze medium: 2-ounce bottle

* Glitter: ultra-fine green

* Lint-free cloth

* Paintbrushes:
    1" craft
    No. 6 round

* Paring knife

* Plastic spoon

* Ultra-fine permanent marker: black

* White craft glue

Trimming Figure

★ Holding paring knife at a 45-degree angle, trim seams formed from molding process. Figure should be damp but quite firm.

Drying Figure

★ Place figure in 200-degree oven 3–4 hours, or until completely dry.

Painting Figure

★ *Using 1" craft brush:* Paint vase with two coats of periwinkle, avoiding bunnies and base; dry between coats.

★ *Using No. 6 round brush:* Paint each bunny white with pink ears; small triangular pink nose; bright emerald green grass along base, avoiding bunny toes.

Glazing Figure

★ Mix 2-ounce bottle of faux glaze, 2 ounces of water, and ¼ teaspoon of raw umber paint in small jar. Using lint-free cloth, gently rub figure with mixture; let air dry 2–3 hours. Draw whiskers and eyes on each bunny with black marker.

Glittering Figure

★ Dilute 2 tablespoons of white craft glue with ⅛ teaspoon of water and apply to entire piece using 1" craft brush. Sparsely sprinkle with green glitter.

Adding Finishing Touches

★ Insert small drinking glass or jar into container and fill with luscious home-grown summer flowers.

Faithful Companion Named Joey

This dog, Joey, is made from a vintage metal mold and is a celebration of all mixes and breeds. He could be a small version of Nana from the nursery in the J.M. Barrie tale of *Peter Pan*, or a Burmese Mountain dog. Each one is a wonderful version of man's best friend.

Dogs are dear to my heart. My family has rescued nine dogs in less than ten years. Two of the dogs were abandoned and turned themselves in directly to me. Callie was found wandering a highway near a tiny town in Texas; Jake the junkyard dog is from Virginia; and the others arrived through a variety of ways.

My collection of vintage papier-mâché dogs grew just a little faster than my collection of real dogs.

Materials

* 4"x6" silicone dog mold
* ¼" velvet ribbon: rose (4")
* Acrylic paint:
    black
    brown
* Cooking spray
* Dry papier-mâché mix: 2 cups
* Fabric scissors
* Glitter: ultra-fine gunmetal
* Hot-glue gun and glue sticks
* Instant age varnish: 2-ounce bottle
* Latex paint: white
* Lint-free cloth
* Mold clips or rubber bands: small (2)
* Paintbrush: No. 5 round
* Paring knife
* Tiny bell
* Ultra-fine permanent marker: black
* White craft glue

Instructions

Open mold and lightly spray with cooking spray. With fingers, rub spray to reach all crevices and remove any accumulation in the details.

Shaping Figure

* *To make slurry:* Combine 1 cup of dry papier-mâché mix and 1 cup of water in bowl; mix thoroughly. Place half of mixture in each side of mold; press into details and up the sides just short of the top. Let dry about 30 minutes until slightly firm but still wet.

* *To make second layer:* Mix 1 cup of dry papier-mâché mix with ½ cup of water. Use this thicker mixture to finish filling the mold, overfilling just a bit. Stand mold upright, securing with mold clips. Let set 45 minutes, until firm.

* Pry in a few spots along side of mold with a paring knife. Remove half of mold. If figure has details that are missing, repair. If they are simple, sculpt with paring knife. If figure is missing more serious details, add wet papier-mâché scraps and replace mold for 10 minutes. Repeat as necessary.

Trimming Figure

* Holding paring knife at 45-degree angle, trim seams formed from molding process. Figure should be damp but quite firm.

ARTIST'S *notes*
An Antique Touch

A dog may be glittered with any of the wide assortment of glitters available. I save snow and sugary effects for other seasonal figures. My dogs are often accented with one of my antique metallic glitters. Sometimes I choose to use no glitter at all. When this choice is made, a golden glaze will give a new papier-mâché piece a lovely aged patina.

Drying Figure
✶ Place figure in 200-degree oven 2–4 hours.

Painting Figure
✶ Paint body of dog with white latex paint; let dry. Referring to project photo, paint an irregular shape on dog's side brown. Paint ears, areas around eyes, and elongated space between ears black. Paint tiny half-moon eyes brown.

Glazing Figure
✶ Using lint-free cloth, rub instant age varnish over entire dog to create patina; let air dry 30 minutes.

Glittering Figure
✶ Apply undiluted white craft glue to two patches between dog's eyes and highlights along top of brown patches on his sides using paintbrush. Sprinkle on heavy layer of glitter.

Adding Finishing Touches
✶ Using black marker, draw whiskers and claws. Apply undiluted white craft glue to accent areas, including the legs, ears, nose, and selected spots along the back using paintbrush. Sprinkle these areas with glitter.

✶ Cut velvet ribbon to fit around neck as a collar. String bell on ribbon. Carefully tuck end under on one side and hot glue in place. Overlap ends about ½" on dog's neck and hot glue in place.

Bridal Wedding Topper

This gorgeous couple seems to be from the late-Victorian era. There is a lovely set of vintage metal molds for this couple made in several sizes. Since papier-mâché is so corrosive to metal, I use plastic molds similar to the originals.

Using the silicone mold-making technique, I have made bridal couples from the 1950s and '60s. The original bride and groom figure was celluloid or plastic. Plastic figures allow me to make silicone molds in amazing clarity.

Instructions

Separate two-part mold; lay halves with interiors facing up on workspace.

Shaping Figure

★ Combine 1 cup of water and 1¼ cup of dry papier-mâché mix in large bowl; mix thoroughly, removing all clumps. Pour about half of mixture into each half of open mold, laying both cavity side up on work surface. Push wet mixture into details and completely fill mold just over top edge. Place mold sides together and press firmly. Stand the bride on her feet. Secure closed with rubber band; let set 30 minutes or until firm.

Trimming Figure

★ Remove rubber band and gently pry top half of mold away from figure using paring knife. With figure facing up, carefully repair any missing or incomplete details with leftover papier-mâché mixture. Press mold firmly over repairs, repeating as necessary. Temporarily replace top half of mold while repairing second side.

★ With both sides of mold removed, stand the bride on her feet. If not flat, add damp papier-mâché scraps so she stands correctly. Holding paring knife at 45-degree angle, trim seams formed from molding process.

Drying Figure

★ Place in 200-degree oven 4–5 hours.

Materials

* 1¼"-wide satin ribbon
* 7" plastic bride and groom mold
* Acrylic paint:
    black
    brown
    golden yellow
    light peach
    pale mint green
    pale pink
    raw umber
    red
    white
    yellow
* Dry papier-mâché mix: 4 cups
* Faux glaze medium: 2-ounce bottle
* Glitter: crystal
* Hot-glue gun and glue sticks
* Lily of the valley wired garland, sprig
* Lint-free cloth
* Paintbrushes:
    1" craft
    No. 5 round
* Paring knife
* Piercing tool
* Rubber band: medium
* Scissors:
    craft
    fabric
* Ultra-fine permanent marker: black
* Vintage-style wedding paper
* White craft glue

Drying & Shaping Figure
The Groom
✱ Repeat all steps from the bride, placing him in the oven alongside his bride. Check both for doneness in several hours. Figures should be lightweight and feel dry to the touch. The groom's feet are small so spend a few minutes making him stand in a stable manner by adding damp papier-mâché scraps and flattening bottom of shoes before drying him.

Painting Figures
The Bride
✱ *Using No. 5 round brush*: Paint veil, socks, shoes, and dress white; let dry. Paint face, arms, and legs light peach. Load brush with pale pink paint and dip just the tip in red. Paint tiny flowers, forming a subtle rose color for the flowers around her veil. Repeat this process for the bouquet of roses and single rose the bride is holding. Paint tiny yellow centers in all flowers and pale pink bows on shoes. Dip tip of brush into yellow and then load brush with white right on top of the yellow. Apply little dots to pearl necklace. Paint hair golden yellow and add a red mouth and pale pink cheeks. Accent shoes and socks with pale mint green.

The Groom
✱ *Using No. 5 round brush:* Paint hands and face light peach and hair brown. Paint mouth red and cheeks pale pink. Mix 1 drop of black paint with a dab of white paint to make gray and paint hat and trousers. Paint coat black and vest a mixture of equal parts of white and pale mint green paint; paint tie pale mint green. Paint shirt white and shoes black, and then add a pink boutonnière. Add six tiny white buttons down vest with freshly pointed brush.

Platform for Topper
✱ Cut 4"x 8" piece of wedding wrapping paper and set on work surface, printed side down.

✱ Hand-mix 1½ cup of dry papier-mâché and ¾ cup of water, adjusting as necessary to achieve a sculpting consistency. Form a small, flat platform 2"x 5½"x ½" using your fingers and knife on top of the wedding paper. When papier-mâché is firm, turn wrapping paper side up and gently tear away excess paper.

Drying & Painting Platform
✱ Place platform in 200-degree oven 2 hours. When dry and cooled, paint sides white using No. 5 round brush.

Applying Glaze
✱ Combine 2-ounce bottle of faux glaze medium, 2 ounces of water, and ¼ teaspoon of raw umber paint in small bowl; mix well. Using lint-free cloth, rub figure with mixture; let dry thoroughly.

Adding Finishing Touches & Glittering Figure
✱ Draw eyes and eyebrows using black marker.

✱ Avoiding the faces, apply undiluted white craft glue using 1" craft brush and then cover with crystal glitter.

✱ Hot-glue bride and groom to platform, placing groom on the bride's right to allow more space for his top hat.

✱ Using piercing tool, carefully puncture the platform at either end (don't go all the way through base). Insert wired garland ends into each hole, forming an arch. Secure with a dab of hot-glue at each end.

✱ Casually place a sprig of lily of the valley on platform as shown in photo. Cover the stand with white craft glue using 1" brush and then sprinkle with crystal glitter. Add white craft glue and crystal glitter to garland and flowers on the stand, if desired.

✱ Hot-glue ribbon in between garland. Make a hem by wrapping ends of ribbon around the wire, hiding unfinished edges in the back and securing with hot-glue.

Chapter 4

Autumn

The colors of autumn are distinctive and brilliant, nothing soft, pastel, or shy about this palette. Follow nature's lead and you will never be wrong when combining colors. Brilliant crimson on a maple leaf dappled with the most amazing greens or the rich terra cotta of bittersweet and pumpkin alongside the brilliant reds of scarlet and crimson are some of my favorites. Stop at a roadside flower stand or plant zinnias in the summer. They are in their full glory in the early months of autumn.

When glittering autumn figures, I choose dustings of gold, gunmetal, and coppery glitter to shimmer and flicker by the light of the fire in the fireplace.

I want to get out my paints when I think of a Washington Irving night with a pale-yellow moon and indigo sky, full of spooky sounds and walks in crisp leaves that cast a spell that can only occur in these late months of the year.

My turkey projects are beautiful in the early dark evenings of the season glimmering by candlelight, with friends and family gathered. From my studio to your home, I invite you to take your time, experiment, and enjoy the process of creating autumn-inspired figures.

Bountiful Harvest Turkey Centerpiece

The richness of the fall colors in this exceptional turkey is absolutely luscious—deep semi-sweet chocolate brown, garnet red, vineyard green, and burnt orange. I also add autumn gold and an unexpected touch of blue. This turkey is an advanced project, made with a three-part mold. He is so big that I need to make certain he is completely dry so I bake him at least 24 hours. There are many shapes and sizes of turkey molds. You can never have too many turkeys.

Materials

* 9½" x 30" three-part turkey mold

* Acrylic paint:
    avocado
    black
    brown
    garnet
    gold
    harvest orange
    metallic gold
    olive green
    pale blue
    raw umber

* Dry papier-mâché mix: 32 cups

* Faux glaze medium: 2-ounce bottle

* Glitter: ultra-fine gold

* Lint-free cloth

* Mixing spoon: large

* Paintbrushes:
    ⅜" flat
    1" craft
    No. 0 round liner
    No. 5 round

* Paper clips: large (4)

* Paring knife

* Rubber bands: extra large (4)

* White craft glue

Instructions

Lay three parts of mold on working surface, interiors facing up.

Shaping Figure

★ *To make slurry:* Combine 3 cups of dry papier-mâché mix and 2 cups of water in large bowl; mix thoroughly, removing all clumps.

★ Using large mixing spoon, ladle wet mixture into all three parts. Place enough wet papier-mâché in tail to fill all feather details. You need to keep the wet mixture below the top edges, where mold parts meet. Do not continue up to top edge of tail section.

★ Add remaining wet mixture, spreading evenly in mold. This will be quite wet. Pull mixture almost to top edge of mold. Press with your fingers to help it sink into all details; let set 45 minutes.

★ *To make second layer:* Combine 6 cups of dry papier-mâché mix and 3 cups of water in large bowl; mix thoroughly, removing all clumps. This will be thicker than previous mixture. Spoon into sides as above, not continuing to any top edge with wet mixture. Continue with this process, mixing about 5 cups of papier-mâché mix and 2½ cups of water at a time until you have used a total of 24 cups of dry papier-mâché mix and 12½ cups of water.

★ Combine 5 cups of dry papier-mâché mix and 2½ cups of water in large bowl. Working quickly, fill in both sides and tail section to a bit over top edge of mold; press down firmly on mixture.

★ Quickly place three mold parts together. Secure tail to body with large paper clips, sides closed with rubber bands, and stand mold upright; let set about 1 hour. Bottom may need additional wet papier-mâché at this point to make a smooth surface.

* Lay mold on work surface. Gently loosen one side of mold by prying with paring knife; remove top half. Taking damp papier-mâché that has been squeezed from the mold, repair any missing parts or details that were missed. If figure requires major repairs, make extra mixture with 1 part dry papier-mâché mix, 1 part water; fill in missing details and press back into the mold. Stand mold on work surface and repeat with other half. Repeat with tail section. Wait about 5 minutes and check again. Head and neck will be delicate. Repeat if necessary. This turkey has a delicate neck and the back may have settled; simply fill in any part with fresh or damp mixture and replace mold.

Trimming Figure

* Holding paring knife at 45-degree angle, trim seams formed from molding process, taking care around the head. Figure should be damp but quite firm.

Drying Figure

* Place figure in 200-degree oven for about 24 hours. *Note:* Pieces dry from the outside in and therefore moisture sometimes remains in the center of a seemingly dry piece, especially a large piece. Place the figure on a surface that will not be affected by moisture for a few days after all procedures.

Painting Figure

* *Using No. 5 round brush:* Paint head and wattle garnet and base avocado; turkey's toes with horizontal orange stripes, overlapping just a bit. On a small dish, squeeze small puddles of brown, gold, olive green, pale blue, and garnet. Wipe excess from brush but retain a touch of the last color used.

* *Using ⅜" flat brush:* Paint top of turkey's back garnet with enough orange to spice it up a bit; small top

grouping of embossed feathers on each side brown; next group of embossed feathers pale blue.

* *Using No. 5 round brush:* With brush still unrinsed, dip into avocado and paint third section of feathers. Paint small section of feathers on front side orange.

* *Using ⅜" flat brush:* Paint lowest sweeping feathers on wing garnet; back section of wing gold; continue with gold around side and back feathers. Paint tail brown upwards from body of bird all the way to the tips. Add indistinct band of gold on the top of brown. Paint final top section of tail feathers garnet, zigzagging a bit to make indistinct sections, using photo for reference. The only mistake you can make is to paint with too much structure and rigidity. Turn bird around and finish back section. Paint back of tail garnet and middle section olive green.

* *Using 1" craft brush:* Paint solid part of tail olive green and brown and large turkey breast olive green.

* *Using No. 0 round liner brush:* Paint turkey's eyes black; let air dry.

Applying Glaze

* Combine 2-ounce bottle of faux glaze, 2 ounces of water, 2 tablespoons of metallic gold paint, and 1 teaspoon of raw umber paint in small jar; mix well. Using lint-free cloth, gently rub figure with mixture; let air dry 30 minutes. *Note:* The glaze will further blend the colors, making them more cohesive and giving the turkey a lovely patina.

Glittering Figure

* Dilute ½ cup of white craft glue with 2 tablespoons of water. Using 1" craft brush, sparingly brush glue mixture over entire turkey. Lightly sprinkle with gold glitter.

Jake the Cocker Spaniel

There's nothing more refreshing than spending an afternoon walking through the fallen leaves with a faithful dog. My entire life has been sweetened by the dogs we have found here and there and the ones that have found us. The original for Jake was a vintage chalkware pup I found at a thrift store. His face was so incredibly engaging and loveable that I couldn't resist. I knew he would be a wonderful addition to my papier-mâché dog collection, so I made a mold. We will give him glitter accents like the old carnival chalk pieces.

Instructions

Separate two-part mold; lay halves with interiors facing up on workspace.

Shaping Figure

★ *To make slurry:* Combine 1 cup of dry papier-mâché mix and 1 cup of water in large bowl; mix thoroughly, removing all clumps. Partially fill each mold half; let set at least 30 minutes.

★ Combine 2 cups of dry papier-mâché mix and 1 cup of water; mix thoroughly and complete filling of mold halves. Press mixture firmly into mold, just over top edge, and place sides together.

★ Place rubber band around mold and lay open-side down on work surface; let set at least 30 minutes. Check open bottom for firmness.

★ *To remove figure:* Using paring knife, gently pry in several spots until you feel mold pulling away from figure; remove half of mold. If mold does not pull away, let figure dry a few more minutes.

★ Hold mold in your hand on its side and remove either half, leaving figure in other half of mold for support. Make any repairs necessary on the open side. Press figure back into mold for missing features or details, if necessary. Turn mold over and repeat with other half.

Trimming Figure

★ Holding paring knife at 45-degree angle, trim seams formed from molding process. Figure should be damp but quite firm.

Materials

* 8" dog figure
* Acrylic paint:
    black
    metallic gold
    pale golden brown
* Dry papier-mâché mix: 3 cups
* Fabric scissors
* Gel mold (see Making Gel Mold technique, page 20)
* Glitter: ultra-fine gunmetal
* Hot-glue gun and glue sticks
* Lint-free cloth
* Paintbrushes:
    1" craft
    No. 0 round liner
    No. 5 round
* Paring knife
* Rubber band: medium
* Tiny bell
* Vintage velvet ribbon: olive green (6")
* White craft glue

Drying Figure

✴ Place figure in 200-degree oven 3–5 hours; let cool and check for dryness.

Painting Figure

✴ *Using 1" craft brush:* Paint body of figure pale golden brown; dry completely.

✴ *Using No. 0 round liner brush:* Paint eyes and nose black and add whiskers and separation of toes.

Glazing Figure

✴ Mix ¼ cup of water with 1 tablespoon of metallic gold paint in small jar. Using lint-free cloth, rub glaze in all details to create aged appearance; let air dry about 30 minutes.

Glittering Figure

✴ While figure is still wet from glaze, sprinkle glitter on legs, paws, nose, ears, and the top of head with glitter. Paint small streaks with No. 5 round brush and undiluted glue to accent ears, legs, chest, and top of head. Sprinkle these areas heavily with glitter.

Adding Finishing Touches

✴ Hold ribbon next to dog for measuring. (You can't go over ears so the collar is done in two pieces.) For front section of collar, thread an old-looking bell onto the ribbon. Hold ribbon between ears and cut to fit. Hot-glue ribbon in place with a dab on the underside of each end. Repeat, without bell, for back of collar.

ARTIST'S notes
An Artful Arrangement

I like to display my collection of dogs on a shelf in my antique butternut cupboard. Many are my own creations, mingling with several metal dogs that once belonged to my mother. The mellow colors of old books enhance a vignette designed for just about any season.

Vintage glass ornaments, antique pink lusterware, and printed-paper pieces from the past add charm to papier-mâché figures. In December, a snowbaby looks nostalgic sitting next to a worn sisal tree under a glass cloche with a little snow glitter sprinkled around his feet. That same figure can be placed on a milk glass cake stand alongside a vintage valentine and displayed in February, perhaps sitting on a new paper doily.

I use glass cloches to add a touch of magic to a solitary piece or to enclose a little scene for any season, such as a faded blown-glass ornament lying on its side next to a papier-mâché snowman with a scarf in similar hues.

I use all types and heights of old cake stands—milky white glass with fancy, lacy edges, elegant cut crystal, or plain old-fashioned pressed glass create a striking display.

Turkey Place Card Holder

A gathering of family and friends would surely be welcomed with their name perched on a hand-crafted turkey place card holder in warm autumn tones. Guests can be mingled in new and different ways to spark conversation.

For this turkey, we use a gel mold to make the small figure. The original figure, made in great numbers a few decades ago, was made from a hollow papier-mâché smoothed with a thin layer of plaster. Many can still be found in antiques shops, and over the years I have snapped up many of these little turkeys. I used one of these originals to create a gel mold, and I can make multiples from this single mold.

Insert a brass paper clip into each turkey before drying, which will be used to hold the place card. I like to paint each bird uniquely but within the same color family.

Instructions

Open mold and lay face up on your work surface.

Shaping Figure

★ Combine ⅛ cup of dry papier-mâché mix and ⅛ cup of water in small bowl; mix thoroughly, removing any clumps. Pour wet mixture into mold cavity. Be certain papier-mâché is well settled into head and neck; wait 5 minutes. Turn mold over and place on work surface; let set about 30 minutes. Check bottom of turkey, it should be damp and firm.

★ Pry mold from figure using paring knife, one side then the other. Repair any missing details, reshaping any features that are incomplete using leftover partially set papier-mâché and paring knife. If necessary, place back in mold about 2–3 minutes.

★ Insert smaller end of brass paper clip halfway into turkey, forming card holder.

Drying Figure

★ Place figure(s) on cookie sheet in 200-degree oven 2 hours.

Materials

- 2" vintage turkey figure
- Acrylic paint:
  avocado
  brown
  gold
  metallic gold
  orange
  pale blue
  pale green-blue
  red
- Brass paper clip: large (1 for each figure)
- Cookie sheet
- Craft knife
- Dry papier-mâché mix: ¼ cup for each figure
- Gel mold (see Making a Gel Mold technique, page 20)
- Glitter:
  ultra-fine copper
  ultra-fine gold
- Heavy cardstock: off-white
- Lint-free cloth
- Paintbrushes:
  1" craft
  No. 5 round
- Paper towel
- Paring knife
- Scallop-edge scissors
- Ultra-fine permanent marker: black
- White craft glue

Painting Figure

* *Note:* I have only four guidelines for painting these turkeys. The tips of the tail, head, and waddle are always red and base is avocado. Remaining paint colors can be used at your discretion. Ideas for your first turkey:

* *Using No. 5 round brush:* Paint head and wattle red and tail feather tops gold, keeping tip of brush pointed; paint top of back brown and base avocado. Rinse brush and dab on paper towel. Dip in pale green-blue paint and paint the feather section between the body and the gold tail feathers. Wings are in three rather indistinct sections. Next to breast, paint gold, then moving back towards rear, paint tiny section pale green–blue. Paint final section of wing orange. Paint back of turkey: lower area brown, large middle section pale bluish green, and top gold. Add tiny trim of red to tips of tail feathers.

* Add three tiny toes on each side by dipping tip of brush in orange and adding little stripes using No. 5 flat brush.

Glazing Figure

* Mix 1 tablespoon of water with 1 teaspoon of metallic gold paint in small jar. Using lint-free cloth, rub entire turkey with mixture; let air dry 30 minutes. When dry, add dot for eyes with marker.

Glittering Figure

* Mix ⅛ teaspoon of copper glitter with ⅛ teaspoon of gold glitter. Dilute 2 tablespoons of white craft glue with ½ teaspoon of water; mix well. Using 1" craft brush, brush over entire turkey except bottom of base. Cover completely but sparingly as dried glue can be visible on dark colors. Immediately sprinkle lightly with glitter mixture.

Adding Finishing Touches

* Using scallop-edge scissors, cut 3"x 2" place card for each turkey from heavy cardstock. Write name and insert in place card holder.

ARTIST'S notes
Slow Drying Time

All homemade papier-mâché recipes have long drying times. Some recipes use cloves or bleach to disguise the sour odor. Some pre-made dry mixes sold in crafts stores also have slow drying times. This project does dry at a snail's pace and can't be removed from the mold until the figure is firm enough to keep its form. I love the result but the process requires patience.

Mama Cat and Her Baby

I love dogs but would like to give equal space to cat lovers. They can be a lovely addition to an artist's studio, offering quiet, detached companionship and making few demands on the owner. My family has no cats but the ease of care is certainly appealing.

This pair is very sweet and devoted. Mama is a very maternal figure of love grooming her kitten. I have owned a beeswax figure of this pair for many years. This was undoubtedly made from an old metal mold, which I have never seen so I made my own mold from the original figure. At 4" tall, I admired the original for the fine detailing. Even the tiny tongue comes through quite clearly. Mama Cat would be lovely displayed with a ball of vintage yarn, sitting on an old book.

Materials

* 4" beeswax mother and cat figure

* Acrylic paint:
  black
  brown
  burnt umber
  red
  white

* Dry papier-mâché mix: 1¾ cup

* Fabric scissors

* Faux glaze medium: 1 ounce

* Glitter: ultra-fine copper

* Paintbrushes:
  1" craft
  No. 0 round liner
  No. 5 round

* Paring knife

* Rubber band

* Silicone mold (see Making a Silicone Mold technique, page 21)

* White craft glue

Instructions

Open mold halves and lay face up on work surface.

Shaping Figure

* Combine 1¾ cups of dry papier-mâché mix and ½ cup of water; mix thoroughly, removing all clumps. Fill just over top edge of cavity with wet mixture. Press mixture firmly with fingers, remembering where tongue depression and ears are located, to fill details of mold. Place mold pieces together and squeeze. Turn mold upright so opening is on bottom and place on work surface.

* Secure mold closed with rubber band; let set about 45 minutes, until bottom of figure is firm. Pry mold from figure with fingers and paring knife. Using wet leftover papier-mâché mixture, repair any missing sections of cats.

Trimming Figure

* With tiny features like the noses and tongues, repairs will almost certainly be required. Sculpt a bit with a paring knife after piece is finally removed to make certain the ears are pointy and other features are well shaped.

* Using paring knife, carefully define kitten's face, mom's tongue, and other fine details, referring to photo of project. Using paring knife, trim seams formed from the squeezed papier-mâché.

Drying the Figure
* Place figure in 200-degree oven about 2–3 hours.

Painting Figure
* *Using No. 5 round brush:* Paint entire piece white, using photo of project as your guide for the coloration. Paint a few tiny stripes of brown on Mama cat's tail; accent with thin black, randomly placed stripes.

* *Using No. 0 round liner:* Paint hair on back with fine strokes of brown; inside of her ears, nose, and tongue red; draw eyes and whiskers on both shapes when all paint has dried with liner brush and black paint. Accent ears on both cats with black. Paint a minimum of tiny stripes of black fur from outside of cheeks, continuing to back. Smudge with finger while wet.

Glazing Figure
* Mix 1 teaspoon of burnt umber paint, 1 ounce of faux glaze medium, and 1 ounce of water in small jar. Apply glaze over entire figure using 1" craft brush, highlighting all details.

Glittering Figure
* Dilute ¼ cup of white craft glue with 1 teaspoon of water; apply to figure using 1" craft brush. Sprinkle immediately with light layer of copper glitter.

Pumpkinhead Ghost

A ghost was one of my favorite Halloween costumes, and not because of the ease of cutting eye holes in an old cotton sheet. It was because of the complete anonymity of becoming a Halloween ghost, no pigtails or hints of the identity of the little trick or treater.

My collection of seasonal goodies includes a few boxes of new and vintage Halloween items—thin streamers with spooky designs and printing, twigs from my garden, tiny sisal brooms, skulls, and little books filled with potions and spells.

This project is great for the beginner and combines many fun embellishments. When autumn arrives, check out craft and party stores for cool accessories, such as key chains or party favors. Use your creativity to imagine what a new item could look like with minor changes.

Instructions

Cut paper towel roll into 3" piece. Cover one with sandwich bag held by a rubber band; discard extra. The cardboard tube is covered with the plastic so it will hold its shape and not become soggy. It is the core for your figure.

Shaping Figure

* Combine ½ cup of water and 1 cup of dry papier-mâché mix slowly, removing all clumps. If mix is sticky, dip fingers in water and then work again with papier-mâché mix; repeat as necessary to achieve sculpting consistency.

* Apply papier-mâché mix to the outside of tube until a ghostlike shape forms.

Stand form upright; roll golf ball-size lump of papier-mâché. Place on top of tube and smooth onto ghost's body.

* *To shape a bat:* Using leftover papier-mâché scraps, roll about 1 tablespoon of damp trimmings into a cylinder about 4" long and a little thicker than a drinking straw. Cut in half with your fingernail and place one half over the other, forming a cross. Flatten slightly and form two little ear shapes from the top by pinching with fingers into ear shapes. The horizontal section forms his wings so flatten slightly and point the ends.

Materials

* 1"-wide orange and black checkered streamers

* Acrylic paint:
    black
    ivory
    metallic gold
    orange
    pale blue
    raw umber
    red
    white
    yellow

* Cardboard box: 8" oval

* Craft scissors

* Dry papier-mâché mix: 1½ cups

* Glitter:
    ultra-fine black
    ultra-fine gold
    ultra-fine green

* Hot-glue gun and glue sticks

* Lint-free cloth

* Paintbrushes:
    1" craft
    No. 0 round liner
    No. 5 round

* Paper towel roll

* Plastic cake decorations

* Plastic sandwich bag, non-zip closure

* Rubber band: small

* Spray adhesive

* Synthetic spider webbing

* Tinsel trim: copper (3")

* White craft glue

ARTIST'S notes
Lightening the Glaze

If the glaze seems too dark, quickly rinse the papier-mâché figure in water to remove some of the color; let figure air dry or place in a 200-degree oven about 30 minutes.

Drying Figure

* Place ghost in 200-degree oven 3–5 hours. Bat will dry sooner but a longer time in the oven will not harm the figure.

Painting Figure

* *Using No. 5 round brush:* Paint entire figure ivory; let air dry. Paint head orange with small inverted triangles continuing into the neckline of his outfit.

* *Using No. 0 round liner brush:* Paint mouth and eyes white; let dry. Paint lips red and form teeth with tiny red lines. Paint black triangle for the nose and outline eyeballs with pale blue and then with black paint. Draw little arrow shapes within a circle of pale blue for pupils. For bat, paint entire figure black; paint eyes yellow and ears orange.

Glazing Figure

* Mix 2 teaspoons of water, ¼ teaspoon of metallic gold paint, and 4 drops of raw umber paint in small jar. Rub on ghost using lint-free cloth to create aged effect; let air dry 30 minutes.

Glittering Figure

* Dilute 2 teaspoon of white craft glue with ½ teaspoon of water; mix thoroughly. Apply to entire figure using 1" craft brush. Sprinkle with gold glitter.

* Repeat steps for diluted glue. Apply to bat using 1" craft brush. Sprinkle lightly with black glitter.

Finishing Touches

* Cut 1"-wide streamer to fit diameter of box lid edge and hot glue in place. Hot-glue ghost figure off to the side on top of box lid. Hot glue embellishments onto the box as shown in project photos. Spray with adhesive and then lightly sprinkle with green glitter.

Spooky Old Owl

A breathtaking owl lives in my pine trees. It is magi-cal to hear her "who-o-o, who-o-o" a soothing, yet quite specific, sound all night long. November is mating season so she is hooting more than usual. I know she is a female due to her size, which is larger than the male. This giant bird has a wingspan of at least 4 feet yet she stays hidden all day. Closing my eyes, I can hear the feathery power of her wings in flight at night.

My vintage Halloween collection is ripe with jack-o-lanterns, witches, and ghosts but there's not an owl in sight. This owl project originates from a ceramic piece I found at a thrift store. I frequently see owl figures made from a variety of materials.

Materials

* ½"-wide black-and-orange paper garland (5")
* 4" x 6½" ceramic generic owl
* Acrylic paint:
  black
  brown
  lime green
  metallic gold
  orange
  yellow
* Dry papier-mâché mix: 2⅓ cups
* Glitter: ultra-fine gold
* Hot-glue gun and glue sticks
* Paintbrushes:
  1" craft
  No. 0 round liner
  No. 5 round
* Paring knife
* Rubber band: medium
* Silicone mold (see Making a Silicone Mold technique, page 21)
* Skull
* White craft glue

Instructions

Open mold and lay face up on your work surface.

Shaping Figure

* Combine 2⅓ cups of dry papier-mâché mix and 1 cup plus 2 tablespoons of water in large bowl; mix thoroughly, re-moving all clumps. Pour approximately half of mixture into each side of open mold. Evenly spread mixture up to top edge. Press mix into details of owl. Overfill a bit so mold halves will merge.

* Place mold halves together and secure closed with rubber band. Stand mold upright; let set about 45 minutes, until bottom is firm yet damp.

* Remove mold by prying around edge with paring knife until you feel less resistance. Pry mold off figure.

* Repair any missing parts by applying leftover partially set papier-mâché mix-ture to features needing repair. Replace mold if necessary, press together, and let set about 3 minutes.

Trimming Figure

* Using paring knife, make hollow inside of owl, forming a sort of container. The hole only needs to be about 2" in diam-eter. Holding paring knife at 45-degree angle, trim seams formed from molding process. Figure should be damp.

97

Drying Figure

★ Place owl in 200-degree oven 2–4 hours until dry.

Painting Figure

★ *Using No. 5 round brush:* Paint the log owl is sitting on brown.

★ *Using 1" craft brush:* Paint entire body of owl black.

★ *Using No. 5 round brush:* Complete painting around eye area black; paint pupils black, large area surrounding eyes lime green, and inside this area yellow.

★ *Using No. 0 round liner brush:* Paint beak and claws orange; draw accent lines radiating in spokes on lime green area black.

Glazing Figure

★ Mix 2 teaspoons of metallic gold paint with ¼ cup of water in small jar. Using 1" craft brush, apply mixture to owl; let dry.

Glittering Figure

★ Dilute 2 teaspoons of glue with 1 teaspoon of water; apply to figure using 1" craft brush. Sprinkle with gold glitter.

Finishing Touches

★ Hot glue small skull on log next to claw. Using white craft glue and 1" craft brush, adhere tiny paper banner beneath owl's feet.

ARTIST'S notes
What in the World is Aubergine?

Authentic Halloween collectibles are rather predictable with their colors of black, orange, and gold. I love to punch up the season's colors with vivid chartreuse, a mix of an almost neon yellow and a bright purple. Aubergine, the gorgeous purply black of an eggplant, takes a witch from witchy to quite elegant. Black seems to tie everything together.

Chapter 5

Winter

There is nothing as beautiful as a fresh, overnight snowfall when all is quiet and still. I feel as if I could stay by the fire in my studio forever.

I love winter because of the long evenings. There seems to be more time for all sorts of beautiful and meaningful projects and quiet family moments. The house smells of gingerbread and the fireplace smolders all day long, creating a calming atmosphere.

All of the seasons appear to me in colors that create actual sensations. Winter contains all shades of white, from the crisp white of a new snowfall to the creamy white of a winter tallow berry. A frosty pale blue alongside a white snowflake is pure magic. Visualizing these shades, I can actually feel the biting sensation of a snow crystal stinging my cheek in a wintry wind.

The antique German glass glitter on Katie's Little Cupcake Bird in this chapter is a frosty aquamarine with accents of sterling silver. I use white sticks from the garden with several projects and gilding, both gold and silver.

Snowbaby Ornament

I love winter, children, and silvery vintage ornaments, and this project delightfully combines all three. You will need a delicate touch and extra patience to create this lovely heirloom.

Start with an old silver glass ornament about the size of an orange. I prefer the soft mellow sheen of an ornament with a bit of age on it. Gather a snowbaby and a few inches of sterling tinsel, and get ready to try the gel mold making procedure. It will be worth the effort for this exquisite piece that will surely be cherished.

Instructions

Open mold and lay face up on your work surface.

Shaping Figure

★ Combine ⅓ cup of dry papier-mâché mix and ¼ cup of water; mix well, removing clumps. Pour and press mixture into mold; let set 30–45 minutes.

Trimming Figure

★ Carefully remove figure from mold. Repair any missing details with paring knife and fingers; place back in mold if necessary. Holding paring knife at 45-degree angle, trim seams formed from molding process. Figure should be damp but quite firm.

★ Remove metal top and wire hoop from ornament; twist ends of hoop with fingers, and press about ½" into top of damp snowbaby. Turn snowbaby upside down and, centering as well as possible, gently press and twirl the raw glass top on the damp bottom, making a mark. This will be your guideline for cutting an opening for joining the new piece with the ornament.

★ Hold upside-down figure firmly in your hand. While supporting sides, very gently carve a hole in the snowbaby to hide silver neck of the ornament. Frequently check size of hole; it should be deep enough to hide at least half of neck. Don't join until snowbaby is dry.

Drying Figure

★ Place snowbaby on cookie sheet in 200-degree oven about 1–2 hours.

Materials

❋ 1½" ceramic sitting snowbaby

❋ 2" gel mold

❋ Acrylic paint:
   ivory
   light peach
   pink
   raw umber
   red

❋ Cookie sheet

❋ Dry papier-mâché mix: ⅓ cup

❋ Faux glaze medium: 2-ounce bottle

❋ Gel mold (see Making a Gel Mold technique, page 20)

❋ Glitter: crystal

❋ Hot-glue gun and hot glue stick: silver

❋ Paintbrushes:
   No. 5 round
   No. 0 round liner

❋ Paper towel

❋ Paring knife

❋ Sterling tinsel (6")

❋ Ultra-fine permanent marker: black

❋ Vintage holly sprig

❋ Vintage ornament: silver (4" round)

❋ White craft glue

Painting Figure

* *Using No. 5 round brush:* Paint outfit ivory; face light peach; mittens red.

* *Using No. 0 round liner brush:* Paint tiny mouth red and tiny cheeks pink.

Glazing Figure

* Mix 1 teaspoon of faux glaze medium, 1 teaspoon of water, and 2 drops of raw umber paint in small jar. Rub on entire snowbaby with a torn half of paper towel; let dry completely. Delicately draw eyes and eyebrows with black marker.

Glittering Figure

* *Using No. 5 round brush*: Paint undiluted glue on snowbaby and cover with crystal glitter.

Adding Finishing Touches

* Cover neck of glass bulb with silver hot glue and immediately insert neck into carved hole in snowbaby. Hide rough section where bulb joins papier-mâché. To do this, apply hot glue on the glass in a circle around the baby and cover the glue with sterling tinsel, circling at least twice.

* Twist stem of holly around handle of paintbrush. Remove brush and glue holly onto bulb as shown.

ARTIST'S notes
Secret to Drawing Eyes

Most of my figures have my signature eyes, little inverted half moons with a dot in the center. Occasionally, I paint big white eyes with a blue center and a dot for Halloween, Easter, or a flirty Valentine figure. An ultra-fine black permanent marker is my favorite tool, both for signing the piece and drawing the eyes and brows.

I have been drawing these simple eyes for so long that I very rarely make a mistake. If the eyes were to be drawn wrong, it could take 2–3 layers of the face color to repair. Try a variety of eyes on paper or a dried ball of papier-mâché to find your favorite style. The key is a steady hand and a face that is completely dry. To use a marker, the papier-mâché, paint, and glaze must be thoroughly dry. Markers are great for whiskers too!

Wintry Trumpeter Swan

I selected this trumpeter because of his lovely winter coloration: pure white with a black beak accented with red. He is glazed with a patina and uses three kinds of glitter. He is elegant with a tiny touch of silver on his black beak, a garnet red for the tiny openings on the top of the beak, and snowy glitter on his feathers.

I love to place him on an oval beveled mirror in the center of my table and surround the mirror with silvery glittered branches and a few silver glittered pinecones. I tie a bright red vintage moiré ribbon around his slender neck, which is accented with tinsel roping. He is lovely on his frozen pond, charming everyone all winter long. This magnificent swan is a challenge and requires some experience but it is well worth the trouble.

Materials

* 9½"x 9" plastic chocolate swan mold

* Acrylic paint:
   black
   garnet
   raw umber
   white

* Cardboard shoe boxes (2)

* Dry papier-mâché mix: 11 cups

* Fabric scissors

* Faux glaze medium: 2-ounce bottle

* Glitter:
   crystal
   ultra-fine dark red
   ultra-fine gunmetal

* Hot-glue gun and silver glue stick

* Lint-free cloth

* Paintbrushes:
   1" craft
   No. 3 round
   No. 5 round

* Paring knife

* Sprig of vintage holly

* Sterling tinsel roping (18")

* Ultra-fine permanent marker: black

* Vintage moiré ribbon: red (18")

* White craft glue

Instructions

Separate two-part mold; lay halves with interiors facing up on workspace. Take note of where swan's feathers end at the top of the figure.

Shaping Figure

★ *To make slurry:* Combine 4 cups of water and 4 cups of dry papier-mâché mix in large bowl; mix thoroughly, removing any clumps. Add a bit of papier-mâché mix if there is water standing above the mixture. Pour about half of the wet mixture into one side of mold. Using fingers, spread over the feathers. *Note:* The top edge of the swan mold without feathers does not need the mixture.

★ Smooth papier-mâché mixture along swan's neck, close to top and bottom edges where mold will be joined, just below edge of mold. *Note:* The second batch will go over the top edge so sides of mold will adhere to each other and leave no gaps.

★ Partially fill tail feathers the same way. If desired, use shoe boxes as support by gently laying each mold half in a box to hold it somewhat level. Repeat with other side of mold; let set 30 minutes.

* *To make second layer:* Combine 7 cups of dry papier-mâché mix and 3½ cups of water in large bowl; mix thoroughly, removing all clumps.

* Overfill neck, tail, bottom edges, and all sections that meet the other mold half. Place the mold halves together and line up the indentations. The walls of the swan should be ¾" to 1¾" thick. Reach in and smooth interior with your fingers; there should be at least 1" of papier-mâché mixture on what will be the bottom of your swan centerpiece; let set about 30 minutes, until still damp but firm.

* With swan still lying on your work surface, pry edges of mold gently with paring knife. Continue around entire mold until you feel it loosen; remove top half. Use extra partially set papier-mâché mixture to make any repairs. If repairs are serious, return swan back to mold, press down gently, and wait 5 minutes. Repeat with second half.

Trimming Figure

* Holding paring knife at 45-degree angle, trim seams formed from molding process while swan is firm but still damp. Be sure to trim bottom seam as the swan will be sitting. Trim around his neck with a delicate hand. On the back and sides, carve off anything above the feather line in a somewhat zigzag pattern.

Drying Figure

* Place figure in 200-degree oven 4–6 hours.

Painting Swan

* *Using 1" craft brush:* Paint exterior of swan white.

* *Using No. 5 round brush:* Paint tip of beak black and garnet.

* *Using No. 3 round brush:* Paint eyes black.

Applying Glaze

* Combine 2-ounce bottle of faux glaze medium, 2 ounces of water, and 1 teaspoon of raw umber paint in small jar; mix well. Using lint-free cloth, gently rub figure with mixture; let air dry 30 minutes.

Glittering Figure

* Dilute 1 teaspoon of white craft glue with two drops of water. Using No. 5 round brush, apply glue evenly but lightly on beak. Carefully sprinkle thick coat of dark red glitter on top of beak. Lightly sprinkle gunmetal glitter on remaining section of beak.

* Apply undiluted white craft glue directly over entire exterior except beak and bottom using 1" craft brush. Sprinkle on crystal glitter.

* Apply undiluted white craft glue on a few areas of white sticks, where snow or ice would accumulate, and heavily glitter these spots with crystal glitter.

Adding Finishing Touches

* Lay ribbon on clean surface and place tinsel roping down its length; tie around swan's neck; trim ends. Hot-glue tiny crown on swan's head; hot-glue vintage holly into side of crown.

Hand-Molded Snow Family

My snow family is ideal for the beginning papier-mâché artist. No molds are needed, just your imagination, a little paint, some papier-mâché mix, and a variety of nostalgic accessories. I can give you guidelines but the project is all yours. I make an entire cast of characters including Mom, Dad, baby sister, little brother, and snowdog.

I use cardboard core as framework, which gives structure and saves on the amount of papier-mâché needed. Only the snow family's snowman is created with three balls, the other members are lumpy cylinders, a hint of shoulders with head and arms added.

Instructions

Cut cardboard tubes into the following pieces: 6" (dad); 5" (mom); 4" (little brother); 3" (little sister) using craft scissors. Cover each with plastic wrap, securing with rubber bands.

★ *To Create Family:* Combine 1 cup of dry papier-mâché mix and ½ cup of water in large bowl; mix thoroughly, removing all clumps and squeezing the mixture with your hands. If necessary, add a bit more dry papier-mâché mix or water for workability.

★ *To Make Snowdad:* Cover 6" tube with papier-mâché mixture, adding a little at a time; continue until length of tube is covered with entire batch of mixture.

Tube should be invisible at this point; if not, add more wet papier-mâché mixture. After tube is covered (snowman should be about 10" around his entire body, about 3½" across), the process is much like building a snowman with real snow; each one should be unique.

★ Make second mixture of papier-mâché with same proportions as above. Form a thick cylinder with shoulders at the top (see photo of project). If there is too much wet mixture for the body of one figure, repeat same process with next covered cardboard core. Wet papier-mâché can be added at anytime, even after piece has dried completely.

Materials

❀ Acrylic paint:
    black
    orange
    red

❀ Cardboard tubes from paper towel rolls (2)

❀ Dry papier-mâché mix: 3–4 cups

❀ Embellishments:
    Dad: cream wool from old sweater, doll ice skates, felt top hat with 2" opening, holly sprig

    Mom: 10 pearls, pink sweater, holly sprig, sisal tree 4" tall with base removed, 6" sterling tinsel strand

    Little brother: pale green sweater

    Little sister: 1" sisal tree with base removed, 5" tinsel strand, pink sweater

    Snowman: 4" sisal broom, 4" twigs painted white (2), small bird, felt hat with 1" opening

    Snowdog: tiny bell, ¼"-wide strip of pink sweater

continued on page 110

* Make third mixture of papier-mâché with 2 parts dry papier-mâché mix, 1 part water. Roll into ball larger than a golf ball, but smaller than a tennis ball. Place on top of the "shoulders" of the emerging snowman. Smooth seam where head and body join with paring knife. If snowman is too thin, add fresh papier-mâché mixture along body for plumpness. Leave surface lumpy; after all, it is a snowman.

* Using paring knife, pull a bit of papier-mâché down from his sides to form slightly "melty" rim at the base. Take a pinch of wet papier-mâché mixture and make a tiny cylinder, about ¼" long. Press on snowman's face to create a little carrot-type nose. Smooth onto face with paring knife.

* *To Form Arms:* Sculpt cylinder by rolling about 4 tablespoon of wet mixture into log shapes. Shape into two ¾" lengths and press onto sides of figure. Smooth shapes onto body with paring knife so they look like arms. Curve slightly at hands. If figure becomes too smooth, add lumpiness by pinching surface gently with fingers.

* *To Create Snowman:* Mix 2 cups of papier-mâché mix with 1 cup of water and form a lumpy ball for bottom of three-part snowman. (This lowest part is a bit bigger than a tennis ball.)

* Refer to photo of snowman and make a second lumpy ball; set on top of first section. Make a third irregular lump for the head, about the size of a golf ball.

* When all three parts are stacked, press down on top just a bit. Insert sticks into sides of figure.

* *To Create Snowdog:* Combine 1 cup of dry papier-mâché mix and ½ cup of water in large bowl; mix thoroughly. Shape into oblong lump about 3½"x 2". Sculpt legs into ½"x 2" log. Turn up end in a paw shape and press onto body. Repeat to create three other legs.

* Guidelines for other family members: Snowmom—body 5" tall, 7" diameter; arms 2½" long; head, golf ball size, Brother—body 3½" tall, 6" diameter; arms 2"-long; head golf ball size, Sister—body 2¾" tall, 7" diameter; rounder than brother; arms 2" long; walnut-size head.

Drying Figure

* Place figure in 200-degree oven 2–3 hours.

* To make the head, mold wet papier-mâché mixture into a ball about the size of a walnut. Pinch the end into a nose and attach to body with a little pressure. Form ears from two marble-size lumps pressed into ear shape with your thumb. Mold small amount of papier-mâché mixture into a stumpy tail and attach.

Painting Figures

* *Using No. 5 round brush:* Paint seven black dots of "coal" for snowman smile; all eyes black; add five "coal" buttons to snowman, two to dad, one to brother, and two to sister.

Materials

continued from page 109

* Glitter: crystal

* Hot-glue gun and glue sticks

* Paintbrushes:
    1" craft
    No. 0 liner
    No. 5 round

* Paring knife

* Piercing tool

* Plastic wrap

* Rubber bands:
    small (4–6)

* Scissors:
    craft
    fabric

* White craft glue

* *Using No. 0 liner brush:* Paint delicate red smile on dad and rest of his family. Paint black eyes and nose on snowdog.

* *Using No. 5 round brush:* Dip brush in orange paint and give each figure a carrot nose; add rosy cheeks by dipping brush into red, rinsing most of paint from brush, and then applying watery color to cheeks.

Adding Finishing Touches

* **Snowdad:** Smash top hat to look weathered and worn and hot glue onto snowdad's head. Cut 1"x 10" strip of cream sweater and hot glue around neck. Hot glue scarf in place and trim to desired length. Tie doll skates together, place over snowdad's shoulder, and hot glue in place. Hot glue sprig of holly to hat.

* **Snowmom:** Cut pink sweater in a triangular shape, 7" wide at base, 4" high. Fold up bottom edge ½", forming ½" rim, and then practice pulling bottom of stocking cap around her head. Tuck one side under the other in the back. Hot glue hat onto her head by applying small line of hot glue around her head and placing underside of hat rim on glue. Apply a line of hot glue on long side of hat and attach opposite side. Pull sides of cap down side of snowmom's head and attach with dab of glue. Hot glue tinsel around neck, then individually apply pearls with hot glue gun on top

of tinsel. Hot glue holly sprig on side of stocking hat. Puncture hole with piercing tool under right hand and insert sisal tree, securing with dab of hot glue.

* **Little Brother:** Cut pale green sweater into triangle, 5" at base, 7" sides, and then follow Snowmom's stocking hat instructions. His hat is taller and pulled straight up for 2½" and then the remainder is allowed to drape with the tip of the hat hot glued to his shoulder.

* **Little Sister:** Cut ½" x 4" strip of pink sweater; hot glue around neck. Hot glue crown of tinsel on top of head. Make small puncture near her hand and hot glue sisal tree into hole.

* **Snowman:** Smash snowman's hat to look weathered and worn and hot glue onto head. Hot glue bird on arm and broom onto the other arm.

* **Snowdog:** Cut strip of pink sweater about ¼" high and 2" long and thread tiny bell onto center. Hot glue in place and trim scarf as necessary.

Glittering Figure

* Using 1" craft brush, apply undiluted white craft glue to figure, hats, and accessorizes and completely cover with crystal glitter.

Jolly St. Nicholas

Jolly St. Nicholas is the delightful, chubby Santa I remember from my childhood. He is the first papier-mâché piece I ever created.

I bought St. Nicholas in chalkware form many years ago at an estate sale just because I loved his face and profile. He wasn't very pretty but I have a lifelong habit of collecting things that inspire me on some level. I made two molds using two types of silicone and I have used them for more than ten years.

This wonderful, traditional Santa has red pants, forest green mittens, and a bright red coat. We will make no apologies for the size of his belly, though it does produce a papier-mâché challenge.

Materials

* 8" silicone mold of Santa figure (see Making a Silicone Mold technique, page 21)

* Acrylic paint:
  black
  bright red
  dark green
  light peach
  metallic gold
  raw umber
  white

* Dry papier-mâché mix: 5½ cups

* Faux glaze medium: 2-ounce bottle

* Glitter: crystal

* Lint-free cloth

* Paintbrushes:
  1" craft
  No. 3 round
  No. 5 round

* Paper towel

* Paring knife

* Rubber bands: medium (2)

* Ultra-fine permanent marker: black

* White craft glue

Instructions

Lay opened silicone mold on your work surface, interior side up.

Shaping Figure

★ *To make slurry:* Combine 2 cups of water and 2 cups of dry papier-mâché mix in large bowl; mix thoroughly, removing any lumps. This slurry mix is meant to be runny to capture detail.

★ Pour papier-mâché mixture into molds, a bit more into the front, deeper belly section than in back half, filling just short of top edge. Press firmly into details. Make certain you have at least 1½" in belly; let set about ½ hour, until firm enough not to slip down if mold is placed upright. If excess water accumulates on top of slurry, dab with a paper towel.

★ *To make second layer:* Combine 3½ cups of dry papier-mâché mix and 1¾ cups of water in large bowl; mix thoroughly, removing all clumps. Do not continue to mix after mixture is rather smooth as this will cause it to set quickly.

★ Continue filling mold to just over top edges. Firmly press both sides together and stand upright. Place rubber bands around mold; let set about 45 minutes. Don't remove mold until open soles of feet feel firm but damp.

ARTIST'S notes
Correcting Mistakes

If any paint gets onto Jolly St. Nicholas' unpainted beard and hair, don't scrape it off. Add touches of white paint to blend in mistakes.

Achieving the right blend for a watercolor effect on cheeks takes a little practice so the paint doesn't run.

---

* Gently pry mold in a few spots using paring knife—you will feel figure separating from silicone. St. Nicholas sometimes comes out of the mold incomplete. Use the extra partially set papier-mâché mixture to make repairs. If he needs more papier-mâché than you have, mix a new batch with 1 part dry papier-mâché mix, ½ part water and repair the belly. Smooth new mix on missing part and return to mold; let set 30 minutes. Carefully smooth new repairs with paring knife.

Trimming Figure
* Holding paring knife at 45-degree angle, trim seams formed from molding process. Check again for missing parts such as a nose and return to mold if necessary. Figure should be damp but quite firm.

Drying Figure
* Place figure in 200-degree oven at least 6–8 hours, until dry.

Painting Figure
* *Using No. 5 round brush:* Paint coat and pants bright red; mittens dark green; boots and belt black.

* *Using No. 3 round brush:* Carefully paint face light peach, painting around the eyebrows. If this is difficult, you can paint eyebrows white after the face is dry. Leave beard, trim on hat, and hair unpainted. Add buckles on the belt and each boot with metallic gold paint and paint mouth red.

* With the lightest touch, use a very pale, diluted pink wash to create rosy cheeks. This can be achieved by rinsing the red paint almost out of your brush and dabbing on cheeks using No. 3 round brush.

Glazing Figure
* Mix ½ teaspoon of raw umber paint, 2 ounces of faux glaze, and 2 ounces of water in small jar. Using lint-free cloth, rub entire figure with glaze; let air dry 30 minutes. Draw eyes using black marker.

Glittering Figure
* Dilute ¼ cup of white craft glue with 1 teaspoon of water. Paint over entire figure except bottom of feet and face using 1" craft brush. Immediately roll in glitter; let dry completely.

Perfectly Simple Angel

The first chalkware angel I made 30 years ago was inspired by an angel candle from my childhood. She is the simplest angel I have ever seen and I think that makes her more beautiful.

I can recall traditional elementary school pageants in the 1950s always performed at night. Each year the pageant needed an angel or two. Selfishly, I cannot remember the parts played by my schoolmates or even if there was a storyline. I do have a fondness for my frequent character, an angel dressed in an ivory satin gown. The best part was that the angel had no speaking part, which was a good fit for me.

Materials

* 7" silicone mold of angel (see Making a Silicone Mold technique, page 21)

* Acrylic paint:
  gold
  ivory
  light peach
  metallic gold
  pink
  raw umber
  red

* Dry papier-mâché mix: 1½ cup

* Faux glaze medium: 2-ounce bottle

* Glitter: crystal

* Lint-free cloth

* Paintbrushes:
  1" craft
  No. 0 round liner
  No. 5 round

* Paring knife

* Rubber band: medium

* Ultra-fine permanent marker: black

* White craft glue

Instructions

Separate two-part silicone mold; lay halves with interiors facing up.

Shaping Figure

* Combine 1½ cup of dry papier-mâché and ¾ cup of water in large bowl; mix thoroughly, removing all clumps.

* Overfill mold a bit with papier-mâché mixture. This is done by filling the figure shape itself and going a little above the edge of the figure so when the mold halves are placed together a bit of the mixture will squeeze out of the sides.

* Secure mold closed with rubber band and stand mold upside down. Smooth bottom with paring knife.

Trimming Figure

* Gently pry off top half of mold while on its side in your hand using paring knife. When mold loosens, remove top. If there are any missing features or missing details, repair by filling in with damp papier-mâché mixture that has squeezed out.

* Replace mold for a couple of minutes to help capture the details. With this mold, often the tops of the wings or shoulder is partially missing. Turn mold over and repeat.

Drying Figure

* Place in 200-degree oven 4–5 hours, or until dry.

Painting Figure

★ *Using No. 5 round brush:* Paint angel's hair gold; wings gold; face and hands light peach; gown ivory.

★ *Using No. 0 round liner brush:* Paint rosebud mouth red and cheeks pink; let dry. Using black marker, draw eyes and eyebrows.

Glazing Figure

★ Mix ¼ teaspoon of raw umber paint, 2 ounces of water, and entire 2-ounce bottle of faux glaze medium in small jar. Using lint-free cloth, apply to entire figure, including the bottom; let air dry 30 minutes.

Glittering Figure

★ Dilute 1 tablespoon of white craft glue with ¼ teaspoon of water. Using 1" craft brush, apply glue to entire figure except the bottom and face. Very sparingly, sprinkle glitter all over figure.

ARTIST'S notes
Pick a Palette

For each season I have a palette in my mind. When this is set, the combinations are naturally formed, though I do like to add an unexpected color.

In autumn, looking down as you walk in crisp fallen leaves, blue would be absent. Train your eye and you just may notice a nearby garden with a second blooming of delphiniums or a lone cornflower.

A surprising blue adds a shot of interest and makes a lovely companion to browns, golds, greens, and vivid oranges. Nothing is as blue as the sky of October.

ARTIST'S notes
Vintage Glass Glitter

Vintage glass glitter of all types and colors are gorgeous on the Cupcake Bird. I rarely use this glitter as it obscures my careful painting; however, on this bird, vintage glass glitter is perfect. Using a craft brush, paint the bird white or the same color as the glass glitter. Press the glitter particles into the glue with your hand and let the figure air dry completely.

Painting Figure
* Paint body, head, tail, and eggs with white latex paint. Add round dots for eyes with black marker.

Glittering Figure
* Apply undiluted white craft glue to entire bird using paintbrush. Roll in aquamarine glitter. Sprinkle on a few specks of red glitter while glue is wet.

Adding Finishing Touches
* Hot-glue one end of sterling tinsel trim on each side of nut cup, forming handle. Insert chenille stems of two vintage ornaments into cup and hot-glue in place. Arch each gracefully (see photo of project). Hot-glue silver nest on top of nut cup, and then add eggs with little bird glued on top.

* Hot-glue paper postcard on forked twig; insert twig behind bird and hot-glue in place. Decorate sisal tree using tinsel strand with ornaments; secure with a bit of hot-glue under each end. Apply spots of craft glue on nut cup and sprinkle with silver glitter.

Tree Confections

These adornments are a delightful winter endeavor requiring just a few art supplies, small amounts of papier-mâché, and the most crucial ingredient of all, lots of imagination.

Making these little ornaments is all about using your hands for the tactile experience. There is a variation in proportion of dry papier-mâché mix to water because paper is affected by humidity. The proportion that works in a heated home in January would be different than on a humid summer day. Instructions for measuring water are pretty concise but the dry mix can be loosely packed or measured like brown sugar by slightly packing.

This project will help you learn about papier-mâché. For hand sculpting, the proportion is about 2 parts dry mix, 1 part water. Mix small amounts, no more than can be formed in less than 30 minutes. Since amounts cannot be made precise, be ready to create a new piece with any of the wet leftovers.

Materials

Instructions yield enough for 8–12 small ornaments

❋ Acrylic paint:
  black
  green
  orange
  red
  white
  yellow

❋ Cookie sheet

❋ Dry papier-mâché mix:
  2 cups

❋ Fine gold or silver cord

❋ Glitter:
  crystal
  ultra-fine yellow

❋ Hot-glue gun and
  glue sticks

❋ Paintbrushes:
  1" craft
  No. 0 liner
  No. 5 round

❋ Paring knife

❋ Sewing needle

❋ Small drinking glass

❋ White craft glue

Instructions

Mix a handful of dry papier-mâché about the size of a golf ball. Add water a little at a time, mixing with one hand and pouring drops of water with the other. Remember, the proportion will be approximately 1 part water, 2 parts papier-mâché mix. When mixture is smooth with no dry spots, and feels like it would hold a shape, try any of the projects below.

Shaping Figure

Stocking

★ Mold toe a tiny bit pointed, the stocking itself about ¾" x 2". Indent top of stocking with your finger, about ½" deep. Using sewing needle, poke small hole in top of back of stocking, big enough to thread with fine gold cord when piece is dry. Place on cookie sheet and dry.

House

★ Mold square about 1½", using a paring knife to straighten sides of house by smoothing from bottom to top, going around each side with the flat part of the knife. Press top of square on two opposing sides with knife, inward to form slanting, triangular roof. Pierce hole in top with needle for hot gluing cord when piece is completely dry.

Swan

★ Flatten piece of papier-mâché by rolling it with a glass, to about ⅓" thickness. Using paring knife, cut swan shape. Pierce hole in top of head.

Candy Cane

★ Roll papier-mâché mixture into tiny log. Turn top in candy cane shape and place on cookie sheet to dry.

Drying Figures

★ Wet papier-mâché will adhere to metal cookie sheet when setting up. After it is firm, however, cookie sheets work well with small pieces. Allow to set up until firm, about 25 minutes, and then pierce a hole in the top of each item for later insertion of gold cord. Insert cord into top of roof; hot-glue in place. Transfer pieces to a cookie sheet and dry in 150-degree oven about 1 hour. Place as many projects as desired on the sheet, spaced ½" apart.

Painting Figures & Adding Finishing Touches

★ Paint larger areas using No. 5 round brush and tiny little details like window panes and stripes using No. 0 liner brush.

★ Using 1" craft brush, apply glue, let dry. When each figure has all of its finishing touches, and is completely dry, thread with gold or silver cord and then tie into knot.

Stocking

★ Paint stocking white with red vertical stripes and a solid red heel and toe. When dry, paint undiluted glue on body of stocking and sprinkle with crystal glitter.

House

★ Paint building white. Dip brush, still wet with white, into black and apply this gray to roof. Add three windows on front of house of yellow; outline windows and panes with black and add black front door. Add same windows on sides and back, two each. Outline eaves with black. Add green shrubbery on both sides of front door. Brush house with undiluted white glue and sprinkle with crystal glitter.

Candy Cane

★ Paint candy cane white and add red stripes. Glitter each with any variety of ultra-fine glitter.

Swan

★ Paint figure white with orange beak, add black eyes. Brush glue sparingly over figure and sprinkle with ultra-fine yellow glitter.

About the Author

Artist Teena Flanner has always surrounded herself with vintage family pieces, softly faded colors, and a warm environment. Now the world-renowned artist has become synonymous with her distinctive vintage figures and ornaments—papier-mâché treasures hand painted and dusted with glitter.

More than two decades ago, Teena began collecting 19th-century molds—ice cream, candle, and candy—whatever struck her fancy. These metal molds became the base for her collection of 300-plus Santas, snowmen, rabbits, snow babies, and other heirloom creations.

In 1991, her passion became her profession.

Her following is devoted and growing. Thanks to almost a decade of continuous licensing of her designs, what started as a home-based business has placed Teena's reproductions in thousands of homes throughout the world. Her originals remain exclusive and limited.

Teena's work has been featured in *Mary Englebreit's Home Companion, Country Living, Southern Lady, and Victoria.* She currently has a showroom at the Atlanta Gift Mart in Georgia.

Teena maintains two homes—one in Norfolk, Virginia, and the other in Elm Grove, Wisconsin, where she has consolidated her studio and spends the majority of her time. Along with her sweetheart, Stephen, Teena's sounding board and informal board of directors continue to be her children—Christopher, Susannah, Katie, and son-in-law Joe.

Acknowledgments

This book is about my passion for papier-mâché, not entrepreneurship; however, I have evolved in papier-mâché because it has been my livelihood, more than a full-time job. When I began, my ideas were unique and had I sought possible mentors, I am certain they would have been non-existent. I have been fortunate to have interesting, distinctive people in my life who bring a different light, a different perspective to whatever is on my mind.

Christopher, my son, designed my large, bright, and warm studio. He supports me from afar with his sound advice, patient listening, and diverse viewpoints. He brings me tranquility and knowledge.

Katie, my effervescent daughter, was an unpaid Jill-of-all-Trades in the early days. She continues to aid me in innumerable ways with her amazing memory and her knowledge of current trends. Her sense of style inspires me. Her husband, Joe, can solve any issue with an idea that would have never occurred to me, while putting a smile on my face. They graciously loan me my grandbaby, Jack, who is truly a delight and provides a brilliant change of pace from writing and creating.

Susannah, my youngest, can enter a room and tackle a situation that has been overwhelming. She is creative, full of life, has a keen artistic ability, and is bursting with energy. She can help me focus when my new ideas are out of control. She is a true friend and a guide.

Stephen, my beloved, has shown endless patience in attempting to instruct me in the use of computers. I am reluctant, yet he never gives up. Thanks to him, I am hesitantly moving forward and could not have written this book without his skills and persistence. His son, Alex, provides levity with his 7-year-old point of view.

My dear friend, Diane, has unselfishly listened to me on numerous long walks, since the early days, when my papier-mâché business was overwhelming.

Metric Equivalency Charts

inches to millimeters and centimeters

inches	mm	cm	inches	cm	inches	cm
1/8	3	0.3	9	22.9	30	76.2
1/4	6	0.6	10	25.4	31	78.7
1/2	13	1.3	12	30.5	33	83.8
5/8	16	1.6	13	33.0	34	86.4
3/4	19	1.9	14	35.6	35	88.9
7/8	22	2.2	15	38.1	36	91.4
1	25	2.5	16	40.6	37	94.0
1 1/4	32	3.2	17	43.2	38	96.5
1 1/2	38	3.8	18	45.7	39	99.0
1 3/4	44	4.4	19	48.3	40	101.6
2	51	5.1	20	50.8	41	104.1
2 1/2	64	6.4	21	53.3	42	106.7
3	76	7.6	22	55.9	43	109.2
3 1/2	89	8.9	23	58.4	44	111.8
4	102	10.2	24	61.0	45	114.3
4 1/2	114	11.4	25	63.5	46	116.8
5	127	12.7	26	66.0	47	119.4
6	152	15.2	27	68.6	48	121.9
7	178	17.8	28	71.1	49	124.5
8	203	20.3	29	73.7	50	127.0

yards to meters

yards	meters	yards	meters	yards	meters	yards	meters	yards	meters
1/8	0.11	2 1/8	0.11	4 1/8	3.77	6 1/8	5.6	8 1/8	7.43
1/4	0.23	2 1/4	0.23	4 1/4	3.89	6 1/4	5.72	8 1/4	7.54
3/8	0.34	2 3/8	0.34	4 3/8	4.0	6 3/8	5.83	8 3/8	7.66
1/2	0.46	2 1/2	0.46	4 1/2	4.11	6 1/2	5.94	8 1/2	7.77
5/8	0.57	2 5/8	0.57	4 5/8	4.23	6 5/8	6.06	8 5/8	7.89
3/4	0.69	2 3/4	0.69	4 3/4	4.34	6 3/4	6.17	8 3/4	8.00
7/8	0.80	2 7/8	0.80	4 7/8	4.46	6 7/8	6.29	8 7/8	8.12
1	0.91	3	0.91	5	4.57	7	6.40	9	8.23
1 1/8	1.03	3 1/8	1.03	5 1/8	4.69	7 1/8	6.52	9 1/8	8.34
1 1/4	1.14	3 1/4	1.14	5 1/4	4.80	7 1/4	6.63	9 1/4	8.46
1 3/8	1.26	3 3/8	1.26	5 3/8	4.91	7 3/8	6.74	9 3/8	8.57
1 1/2	1.37	3 1/2	1.37	5 1/2	5.03	7 1/2	6.86	9 1/2	8.69
1 5/8	1.49	3 5/8	1.49	5 5/8	5.14	7 5/8	6.97	9 5/8	8.80
1 3/4	1.60	3 3/4	1.60	5 3/4	5.26	7 3/4	7.09	9 3/4	8.92
1 7/8	1.71	3 1/8	1.71	5 7/8	5.37	7 7/8	7.20	9 7/8	9.03
2	1.83	4	1.83	6	5.49	8	7.32	10	9.14

Index